DAILY BIBLE STUDY GUIDE

VOLUME IV
THE OLD TESTAMENT PART II

BY DR. DELRON SHIRLEY

2005
REVISED 2009

COVER DESIGN BY JEREMY SHIRLEY

To obtain permission to quote material from this book, please contact:

Delron Shirley
3210 Cathedral Spires Dr.
Colorado Springs, CO 80904
teachallnations@msn.com
www.teachallnationsmission.com

Week: One

Day: Monday

Book: Joshua

Chapter: One

Memory Verse: Eight

Principle: Boldly following the commandments and statutes of the Lord is the key to successful living.

Outline:

Verses 1-5 – After the death of Moses, God spoke to Joshua and promised to be with him just as he was with his mentor.

Verses 6-9 – The conditions necessary for this provision were clearly set forth: the command to be bold was voiced repeatedly and the admonition to live solely according to the laws and statutes of the Lord was expressed explicitly. Complete success was guaranteed if Joshua did so.

Verses 10-15 – Joshua sent messengers throughout the camp to inform the people of God's promises and to rally them to enter the land.

Verses 16-18 – The people swore their allegiance to Joshua and committed themselves to putting to death any who would rebel. They then challenged Joshua to lead them boldly.

Prayer Focus: Lord, as I begin a new year, I ask that You help me to be bold in following Your commandments this year – and for the rest of my life. Amen.

Notes:

Spiritual Journal:

Week: One
Day: Tuesday
Book: Joshua
Chapter: Two
Memory Verse: Eleven
Principle: When we walk boldly in the power of the Lord, no enemy can withstand us.
Outline:

> Verses 1-7 – Rahab, a harlot in Jericho, hid the spies whom Joshua had sent to search out the land.
>
> Verses 8-13 – She expressed the fear that the people of the city felt concerning the people of Israel, knowing that the great power of God was with them. She also begged that the spies would rescue her and her family when the armies returned to take the city.
>
> Verses 14-21 – The spies made an agreement with Rahab requiring that she hang a scarlet cord (which seemed to be prophetic of the blood of Christ) from her window as a sign to ensure her protection during the conquest.
>
> Verses 22-24 – The spies returned to Joshua with a testimony that the people of the land feared the army of Israel because it was evident that the power of God was with them.

Prayer Focus: Lord, help me to walk in a way that will manifest Your power and Your mercy in my life. Amen.

Notes:

Spiritual Journal:

Week: One
Day: Wednesday
Book: Joshua
Chapter: Three
Memory Verse: Five
Principle: We must always live holy and prepared before the Lord because He is always ready to do something miraculous in our lives.
Outline:
> Verses 1-6 – Joshua motivated the priests and the people to begin their conquest of the Promised Land, and he challenged them to prepare themselves for a miracle that was to accompany their initial effort.
>
> Verse 7 – The Lord promised Joshua that this catalytic miracle was to elevate him to the place of respect that Moses had enjoyed in the eyes of the people.
>
> Verses 8-17 – In a miracle that paralleled the opening of the Red Sea before Moses, the flooding Jordan River backed up to allow the entire people of Israel to cross on dry ground when the feet of the priests who carried the Ark of the Covenant touched the waters.

Prayer Focus: Lord, help me expect a miracle every day and to walk so that I am worthy to receive it when it comes. Amen.
Notes:

Spiritual Journal:

Week: One
Day: Thursday
Book: Joshua
Chapter: Four
Memory Verse: Six

Principle: It is important to have special places (such as churches and personal "prayer closets") and rituals (such as communion and baptism) which stand as memorials to remind us of who God is and what He has done in our lives.

Outline:

Verses 1-24 – Joshua had the leader of each of the twelve tribes bring a stone from the bed of the Jordan River and build a memorial which was to serve for generations to come that God had miraculously dried up the river to allow the people to cross as they began their conquest of the Promised Land. This miracle also marked the point at which Joshua was recognized with the same respect as was Moses.

Prayer Focus: Lord, help me to always be mindful to establish and then reverence memorials in my own life so that I am constantly mindful of the graciousness You have shown toward me. Amen.

Notes:

Spiritual Journal:

Week: One

Day: Friday

Book: Joshua

Chapter: Five

Memory Verse: Thirteen

Principle: God is always on the side of those who have entered into covenant with Him.

Outline:

> Verse 1 – The parting of the Jordan River caused great fear to fall upon all the rulers and people dwelling in the Promised Land.

> Verses 2-8 – Because no one had been circumcised during their wanderings in the desert, Joshua circumcised all the men to show that the people of Israel were in covenant with God.

> Verse 9 – Once the covenant was renewed, God removed all the reproach of their time in Egypt and named the place of the circumcision Gilgal, meaning "rolled," as a reminder that the stigma had been rolled away.

> Verses 10-12 – As soon as they had entered the Promised Land, the manna ceased and the people began to eat the produce of the land. Their first meal was a Passover, symbolizing the fact that the God who had brought them out of Egypt was also bringing them into the Promised Land.

> Verses 13-15 – Joshua met the Captain of the Army of the Lord, who verified that the Lord was on their side.

Prayer Focus: Lord, I want You to be on my side, and I realize that the only way to ensure that is to establish and maintain covenant with You; therefore, I pledge myself anew to You today. Amen.

Notes:

Spiritual Journal:

Week: Two
Day: Monday
Book: Joshua
Chapter: Six
Memory Verse: Two
Principle: When God decides to give His people the victory, they will win against all
odds and in the most unconventional ways.
Outline:
Verses 1-20 – The city of Jericho fell before the Israelites when they followed
God's simple, yet unusual, plan of arranging a great procession of priests
with trumpets, the Ark of the Covenant, and the host of Israel to march
around the city once each day and seven times on the last day, followed by
a great shout.
Verses 21-27 – They totally destroyed the city, leaving only the gold, silver,
bronze, and iron that they placed in the house of the Lord. In fulfillment
of the promise made by the spies to Rahab, she and her family were the
only residents of the city allowed to survive.
Prayer Focus: Lord, thank You for Your promise of victory. Help me to always believe
that You do intend me to prosper and help me to always follow Your plan for
receiving Your promises, even when Your plan isn't the conventional way of
doing things. Amen.
Notes:

Spiritual Journal:

Week: Two
Day: Tuesday
Book: Joshua
Chapter: Seven
Memory Verse: Ten

Principle: The Lord does not want His people to moan and groan when difficulties come into their lives; He wants them to hear His Word concerning the situation and then determinedly act according to it.

Outline:

Verse 1 – As an introduction to the upcoming story, this verse explains why the attack on Ai was destined to fail: there was sin in the camp. There is always an underlying reason when things do not work out according to the promises of God. It is never God's fault or inability; the problem usually lies with man's sin or lack of faith – or, as we learned in the book of Job, in a demonic attack.

Verses 2-5 – Confident after their resounding conquest of the city of Jericho, the people of Israel attacked Ai with a fairly small contingency of their forces; however, they experienced a demoralizing defeat at the hands of the people of the tiny city.

Verses 6-10 – When Joshua fell on his face and began to lament before God about the loss, God rebuked him and challenged him to get up with strength and take action.

Verses 11-21 – God not only revealed to Joshua that sin had crippled the people, He also showed him that Achan was the guilty party.

Verses 22-26 – After his confession to having taken gold, silver, and clothing from Jericho, Achan and his entire family were stoned to death. The place of their execution was named the Valley of Achor (meaning "Trouble"), and it was left as a warning memorial.

Prayer Focus: Lord, help me to learn from Achan not to defy Your commandments and from Joshua not to despair in times of trouble but to act with determination according to Your Word. Amen.

Notes:

Spiritual Journal:

Week: Two
Day: Wednesday
Book: Joshua
Chapter: Eight
Memory Verse: Thirty-four

Principle: Israel's defeat at the hands of the men of Ai was followed by their resounding comeback after the sin of Achan was dealt with. This story seems a fitting background for the ceremony in which Joshua reminded the people that God's commandments bring blessings when followed and curses when violated.

Outline:

Verses 1-2 – Now that the sin in the camp had been eradicated, the Lord encouraged Joshua to rise up against Ai and guaranteed him success.

Verses 3-29 – By setting an ambush against the army of Ai, Joshua was able to totally destroy and plunder the city on his second attempt.

Verses 30-35 – Joshua built an altar in the valley between the mountains of Ebal (cursing) and Gerizim (blessing). At this altar, he called the congregation together around the Ark of the Covenant and read to them all the laws of God that Moses had recorded. He emphasized the curses that come when the laws are violated, as well as the blessings that come when they are obeyed.

Prayer Focus: Lord, thank You for Your promise that the laws which were formerly written on tablets of stone can be indelibly etched into my heart so that I will not sin against you and inherit the curses rather than Your blessings. Amen.

Notes:

Spiritual Journal:

Week: Two
Day: Thursday
Book: Joshua
Chapter: Nine
Memory Verse: Fourteen

Principle: Proverbs 6:2 tells us that we can be snared or trapped by the words we speak. Once spoken, words cannot be recalled and all vows – even ones entered into through deception or ignorance – must be honored. We must ask God's counsel before making any binding commitments or authoritative statements.

Outline:

Verses 1-13 – The leaders of the Gibeonites devised a plan to deceive the Israelites into making a covenant with them which would save them from being destroyed when the Israelites invaded their land.

Verses 14-15 – The deceptive plan succeeded because Joshua and the leaders of Israel failed to seek God's wisdom before entering into covenant with the Gibeonites.

Verses 16-23 – When the army of Israel reached the cities of the Gibeonites and discovered that they had been deceived, the Gibeonites begged them to honor the treaty and offered to become slaves for the people of Israel in exchange for being allowed to live.

Verses 24-27 – In order to uphold the integrity of his word, Joshua honored his vow to the Gibeonites and saved their lives.

Prayer Focus: Lord, help me to remember that You gave me two ears and only one mouth as a reminder that I must always be sensitive to listen for Your wisdom before I speak. Secondly, help me to be a person of integrity who will honor my word even when it is costly to me or when I have committed myself foolishly. Amen.

Notes:

Spiritual Journal:

Week: Two
Day: Friday
Book: Joshua
Chapter: Ten
Memory Verse: Twenty-five
Principle: II Corinthians 2:14 says that God always (not sometimes, not maybe, not occasionally – but always!) causes us to triumph (not just get by, not just overcome, not just be declared the winner even though we have suffered great losses in the battle – but to come out triumphantly!)
Outline:

Verses 1-8 – When the king of Jerusalem heard about Joshua's conquest of Ai and the treaty between him and the Gibeonites, he was fearful because the Gibeonites were a mighty army that could be very formidable once united with Israel's forces. Therefore, he called together a league of his neighboring kings to fight against them. The response of the Gibeonites was to call upon Joshua to honor the terms of his covenant with them and send his army to defend them.

Verses 9-15 – After the Lord assured Joshua that he would be victorious, he marched his army all night long and then engaged the enemy forces in an all-day battle, eventually calling upon the Lord to lengthen the day so that he could completely rout the enemy. The Lord answered by causing the sun and moon to stand still, lengthening the daylight by almost a full day. In addition, He sent gigantic hailstones which struck down more of the enemy than fell at the hands of Joshua's fighting men.

Verses 16-27 – When Joshua had completed his conquest of the armies, he executed the five kings and buried their bodies in the cave where they had been captured.

Verses 28-43 – Joshua followed his conquest of the kings by making a great swath through the land to capture the southern territory.

Prayer Focus: Lord, help me to believe and live up to Your promise of overcoming victory in every area of my life. Amen.
Notes:

Spiritual Journal:

Week: Three
Day: Monday
Book: Joshua
Chapter: Eleven
Memory Verse: Twenty-three

Principle: God's ultimate plan is one of peace (that His people and the land rest from war); however, there is often need for aggressive action (conquest of enemy forces which have occupied the promised inheritance of God's people) before this peaceful provision can be realized.

Outline:

Verses 1-18 – When the king of Hazor called the remaining kings into a league to fight against Israel, the Lord directed Joshua to fight, conquer, and destroy their forces.

Verses 19-20 – It was actually within the plan of God that the inhabitants of the land would fight against Israel. Under these conditions, Joshua was justified in all that he did against these people, who would have hindered the people of Israel from obtaining the Promised Land left to them in the covenant God made with their father Abraham.

Verses 21-22 – The Anakim (the giants who scared the ten spies so badly that they came back with an evil report after they surveyed the land) were eliminated from all the land except for a few of the coastal cities.

Verse 23 – Once the land was apportioned as the inheritance of the tribes, there was no more war.

Prayer Focus: Lord, help me not to be afraid to act assertively when I understand that it is within Your will to do so in establishing Your kingdom in the world; however, help me to never be aggressive simply for aggression's sake. Amen.

Notes:

Spiritual Journal:

Week: Three
Day: Tuesday
Book: Joshua
Chapter: Twelve
Memory Verse: Seven
Principle: One key to successful Christian living is found in a happy chorus that some churches and fellowship groups sing: "I went to the enemy's camp and I took back what he stole from me."
Outline:

Verses 1-6 – The kings whom Moses conquered are listed along with the fact that the conquered land was divided as an inheritance among God's people.

Verses 7-24 – The kings whom Joshua conquered are listed along with the fact that the conquered land was divided as an inheritance among God's people.

Prayer Focus: Lord, help me to never be greedy but, at the same time, to never be bashful about demanding that the enemy release to me what rightfully belongs to me as my spiritual inheritance. Amen.

Notes:

Spiritual Journal:

Week: Three
Day: Wednesday
Book: Joshua
Chapter: Thirteen
Memory Verse: Thirty-three
Principle: More than all the physical possessions we could obtain as an inheritance, a personal relationship with God Himself is the most treasured heritage.
Outline:
Verses 1-33 – As Joshua entered into old age, the Lord instructed him to be sure to allot all the tribes their specific inheritances, some of which had already been appointed by Moses and some of which had not yet even been conquered.
Prayer Focus: Lord, thank You for all Your gifts to me, but most of all for the gift of Yourself through Jesus Christ. Amen.
Notes:

Spiritual Journal:

Week: Three
Day: Thursday
Book: Joshua
Chapter: Fourteen
Memory Verse: Nine
Principle: Delay is not denial. We must keep our faith in the promises of God – for He
will fulfill them in His timing, not ours.
Outline:
Verses 1-5 – The Promised Land was divided among the tribes by a
predetermined plan of casting lots.
Verses 6-15 – Caleb requested that he be given the mount of Hebron as his
inheritance. He had desired that parcel since Moses had promised it to him
forty-five years earlier, and he had held on to his faith that he would one
day possess it. Even though he was eighty-five years old at this point,
God gave him the strength and stamina to take the mountain from its
gigantic inhabitants.
Prayer Focus: Lord, help me to never give up my hope or relinquish my faith until I have
obtained the fulfillment of Your promises. Amen.
Notes:

Spiritual Journal:

Week: Three
Day: Friday
Book: Joshua
Chapter: Fifteen
Memory Verse: Nineteen
Principle: The Apostle James taught us that one reason we lack some of the things we need is because we fail to ask for them in faith.
Outline:

Verses 1-12 – The land of Judah was mapped out.

Verses 13-19 – Caleb inherited the region of Hebron, the mountain he had conquered at age eight-five.

Verses 20-63 – The cities inhabited by the families of the tribes of Judah are listed.

Prayer Focus: Lord, help me never to neglect to seek after and possess the promises that You have left for me; at the same time, protect me from greed, as James goes on to warn us that the other common error is asking so that we can consume the promises on ourselves rather than using them as a means of blessing others. Amen.

Notes:

Spiritual Journal:

Week: Four
Day: Monday
Book: Joshua
Chapters: Sixteen and seventeen
Memory Verse: Chapter seventeen, verse seventeen
Principle: In His parable of the talents in Matthew chapter twenty-five, Jesus said that the talents were divided according to the various abilities of the stewards. So it is with all God's blessings: when we show ourselves capable of handling more, He releases more into our control.
Outline:
> Verses 16:1-17:11 – The inheritance of the tribes of the two sons of Joseph was allotted.
>
> Verses 17:12-13 – The Canaanites which were not expelled became servants to the new masters of the land.
>
> Verses 17:14-18 – Because of their great numbers, the people of Joseph were permitted to expand their territory. It is interesting that Joseph's name, meaning "fruitful," symbolically foreshadowed this increase.

Prayer Focus: Lord, help me to increase, not just so I can have more, but so I can know that I will fulfill Your plan for my life and ministry to merit Your commendation, *Well done, thou good and faithful servant.* Amen.
Notes:

Spiritual Journal:

Week: Four
Day: Tuesday
Book: Joshua
Chapters: Eighteen
Memory Verse: Three
Principle: We must realize that the blessings and promises that God has given to us must be claimed and possessed by faith; otherwise, they are like gifts left wrapped under the Christmas tree. Not only is the receiver unable to enjoy the gift; the giver is not able to enjoy the smile on the face of the receiver.
Outline:
      Verses 1-10 – The remaining tribes were encouraged to take hold of their possession.
      Verses 11-28 – Benjamin's inheritance was allotted.
Prayer Focus: Lord, as the author of Hebrews said, I am cautiously concerned that I will fail to enter into the promises that You have left for me.(Hebrews 4:1) Amen.
Notes:

Spiritual Journal:

Week: Four
Day: Wednesday
Book: Joshua
Chapters: Nineteen
Memory Verse: Forty-nine
Principle: Leaders deserve to receive physical blessings from those to whom they have given spiritual blessings.(I Corinthians 9:11)
Outline:

       Verses 1-9 – Simeon's inheritance was allotted.

       Verses 10-16 – Zebulun's inheritance was allotted.

       Verses 17-23 – Issachar's inheritance was allotted.

       Verses 24-31 – Asher's inheritance was allotted.

       Verses 32-39 – Naphtali's inheritance was allotted.

       Verses 40-48 – Dan's inheritance was allotted.

       Verses 49-51 – Joshua's inheritance was allotted.

Prayer Focus: Lord, help me to always show proper respect and honor to those who have blessed me. (Romans 13:7) Amen.
Notes:

Spiritual Journal:

Week: Four
Day: Thursday
Book: Joshua
Chapter: Twenty
Memory Verse: Five
Principle: In Christ, we find our city of refuge from the accuser who would try to bring us under condemnation and judgment. The wonderful thing about our city of refuge is that our High Priest is eternal, so we will never have to concern ourselves about losing our right to His protection.
Outline:
Verses 1-9 – Joshua establishes six cities of refuge according to the instructions left him by Moses in Numbers 35:9-34.
Prayer Focus: Lord, help me to always run to You in my times of fear and danger and remain under Your protection continually. Amen.
Notes:

Spiritual Journal:

Week: Four
Day: Friday
Book: Joshua
Chapter: Twenty-one
Memory Verse: Forty-five
Principle: If God said it, that settles it!
Outline:

        Verses 1-42 – According to Moses' instructions in Numbers 35:1-8, the Levites were given cities to dwell in and land to till even though they were not to inherit a set portion of the land because God Himself was to be their inheritance.

        Verses 43-45 – God fulfilled all His promises to the people of Israel by giving them the land and causing all their enemies to be at peace with them.

Prayer Focus: Lord, thank You that none of Your promises ever falls to the ground unfulfilled, and I grasp with hope and faith all the promises You have left to me, expecting fully that they will be fulfilled. Amen.

Notes:

Spiritual Journal:

Week: Five
Day: Monday
Book: Joshua
Chapter: Twenty-two
Memory Verse: Twenty-nine
Principle: Rumors, suspicions, gossip, and jumping to conclusions are great destroyers; however, serious conflict can be avoided through simple communication and direct discussion of the issues.

Outline:

Verses 1-9 – The two and a half tribes who desired to remain east of the Jordan were given leave to return to their families who were waiting for them across the river.

Verses 10-12 – When rumor that the trans-Jordan tribes had built an altar reached the people west of the river, they reacted with hostility and were ready to go to war against their fellow countrymen.

Verses 13-20 – The leaders of the tribes west of the Jordan handled the issue wisely by responding rather than reacting; they arranged to discuss the issues in a directly confrontational, but non-hostile, manner.

Verses 21-34 – The leaders of the trans-Jordan tribes were able to explain what they had done, and the leaders of the remaining tribes understood that their whole concern was founded on conclusions based upon misinformation and rumor.

Prayer Focus: Lord, help me to never prejudge others or base my attitudes toward them or decisions concerning them on unfounded rumors or gossip. Amen.

Notes:

Spiritual Journal:

Week: Five
Day: Tuesday
Book: Joshua
Chapter: Twenty-three
Memory Verse: Eleven
Principle: In I Corinthians 10:12, Paul warned us that we should carefully watch ourselves to make sure that we don't fall when we think that we are standing securely.
Outline:
>Verses 1-5 – Joshua gathered the people together for his farewell speech in which he recited to them how he had led them into their possession.

>Verses 6-16 – He warned them that they had to continue to keep their guard up or else they could fail to love and serve the Lord. If they disobeyed their covenant, they would suffer God's judgment rather than His blessing. It is interesting that he closed his ministry with the same injunction that was his initial command, *Be very courageous to keep and do all that is written in the Book of the Law of Moses.*

Prayer Focus: Lord, help me to never fail to live by the first principles of righteous living. If they were necessary to gain victory, they are necessary to maintain it. Amen.
Notes:

Spiritual Journal:

Week: Five
Day: Wednesday
Book: Joshua
Chapter: Twenty-four
Memory Verse: Fifteen
Principle: Serving the Lord is an aggressive decision which we must make and determine to follow.
Outline:

> Verses 1-13 – Joshua recited how Abraham came from beyond the Jordan, where he had served pagan gods, and drew a parallel with how the Israelites were coming from beyond the same river, where they had also served other gods. Joshua then called the people to the same kind of covenant dedication that Abraham had made when he possessed the Promised Land.

> Verses 14-24 – When the people responded that they would indeed serve the Lord, Joshua warned them of the penalties which they would incur upon themselves if they failed to honor their vow.

> Verses 25-28 – He framed their pledge in the wording of a covenant that he wrote in the Book of the Law and engraved on a stone memorial altar.

> Verses 29-33 – When the work of bringing the people into the Promised Land and returning Joseph's bones to the land of Israel was completed, both Joshua and the high priest died. At least during the transition period, while the other elders who had served under Joshua remained alive, the people kept their vow to serve the Lord.

Prayer Focus: Lord, help me not only to pledge my life to You but to see that I fulfill my promises. Amen.

Notes:

Spiritual Journal:

Week: Five

Day: Thursday

Book: Judges

Chapter: One

Memory Verse: Two

Principle: As we read this chapter, we notice a distinct difference between the success of Judah and that of the other tribes as they attempted to take the territory allotted to them. We must have the determination of Judah to aggressively possess our promises from God.

Outline:

Verses 1-26 – Judah aggressively took possession of the territory promised to him, leaving only a remnant of the inhabitants in place.

Verses 27-36 – The other tribes left significant settlements of the former residents in place as they attempted to take possession of the Promised Land.

Prayer Focus: Lord, help me to have the faith and courage to take one hundred percent of what You have promised me. Amen.

Notes:

Spiritual Journal:

Week: Five
Day: Friday
Book: Judges
Chapter: Two
Memory Verse: Ten
Principle: It is vital that we keep an ever-keen awareness and remembrance of the goodness and greatness of our God, lest we fail to serve and honor Him.
Outline:

Verses 1-6 – The Angel of the Lord reprimanded the people for failing to fully obey the Lord in His commandment to totally eradicate the inhabitants of the land as they took possession of it. He warned that those who were allowed to remain would become a great scourge to the people.

Verses 7-10 – A flashback to the end of the life of Joshua reminds us that the people of Israel served the Lord as long as Joshua was their leader. It was the next generation who sinned against Him because they did not know the greatness of their God.

Verses 11-23 – In a sort of pre-summary of the book, the author of Judges describes Israel's history as a cycle: disobedience followed by punishment in the form of great oppression by the tribes which were not eradicated from the land, followed by the appearance of a deliver who frees them from their captivity. This deliverance is followed by another identical cycle after the deliverer's death.

Prayer Focus: Lord, help me to make a once-and-for-all determination to serve You and to train up my children so that they will also follow after You rather than fall into bondage as did the people of Israel. Amen.

Notes:

Spiritual Journal:

Week: Six

Day: Monday

Book: Judges

Chapter: Three

Memory Verse: Four

Principle: The difficult situations we face in life can be seen as stumbling blocks or as steppingstones and opportunities for us to prove that we will serve the Lord in spite of the problems.

Outline:

Verses 1-6 – The foreign nations that were not totally eradicated under the conquest of the land proved to be God's litmus test to evaluate the loyalty of His people.

Verses 7-11 – Under Othniel, the people of Israel went through their typical cycle: disobedience, captivity, repentance, deliverance, and freedom.

Verses 12-30 – The pattern was repeated under Ehud, who wrought a great deliverance by his crafty assassination of King Eglon.

Verse 31 – The next judge was Shamgar, who won his place in history through a mighty encounter with the Philistines.

Prayer Focus: Lord, help me to break the cycle of bondage by living always in Your will and, therefore, in Your freedom. Amen.

Notes:

Spiritual Journal:

Week: Six

Day: Tuesday

Book: Judges

Chapter: Four

Memory Verse: Eight

Principle: No task (easy, difficult, or impossible) should be entered into without the wisdom and direction of God.

Outline:

 Verses 1-5 – The cycle of disobedience, bondage, and deliverance came upon the people of Israel again.

 Verses 6-8 – When Deborah, the judge in Israel at that time, called Barak to lead the people in their fight for freedom, he responded that he would not go to battle unless she accompanied him. Though this request can be seen as a sign of weakness, it is likely an indication of wisdom that he did not want to take on such a challenge without God's counsel.

 Verse 9 – Deborah's response that he would not get the recognition for the battle is curious in that he, not she nor Jael, is recorded in the list of the heroes of faith in Hebrews chapter eleven.

 Verses 10-24 – Barak led the Israelites into victory against the Canaanites; however, the deciding blow came at the hands of a woman when she assassinated their general.

Prayer Focus: Lord, help me to never move without Your counsel, but to never use "waiting on the Lord" as a cover-up for cowardice when You have spoken about the direction I am to take. Amen.

Notes:

Spiritual Journal:

Week: Six
Day: Wednesday
Book: Judges
Chapter: Five
Memory Verse: Thirty-one
Principle: Many people think that the Bible teaches that God helps those who help themselves; actually, the biblical principle is that God helps those who cannot help themselves. However, He does expect us to cooperate when He directs us to respond as He moves on our behalf.
Outline:

> Verses 1-5 – Deborah and Barak open their song of victory with rejoicing for the present condition of peace which was won by the Lord's intervention as the people fought bravely, willing to sacrifice themselves for the nation.
>
> Verses 6-9 – The fearful condition of the nation under bondage is described.
>
> Verses 10-11 – The victory report is to be given to those who were not at the battlefront.
>
> Verses 12-18 – Those who responded and fought valiantly in the conflict are praised while those who refused to respond to the battle cry are reprimanded.
>
> Verses 19-22 – Supernatural intervention helped accomplish the defeat of the invading enemy army.
>
> Verse 23 – The reprimand of those who refused to assist is elevated to a curse.
>
> Verses 24-27 – Jael is praised for her courageous single-handed conquest of the general of the enemy army.
>
> Verses 28-30 – The denial expressed by Sisera's mother illustrated the dismay of the Canaanites at their loss before the people of Israel.
>
> Verse 31 – The song ends with the anthem that all the Lord's enemies should be so defeated and that God's people should live in victory and peace.

Prayer Focus: Lord, help me to always rise to every challenge and to never shrink back when You call me to respond. Amen.
Notes:

Spiritual Journal:

Week: Six
Day: Thursday
Book: Judges
Chapter: Six
Memory Verse: Thirteen
Principle: Many people feel that miracles, signs, and wonders are just stories from long ago recorded in the Bible; but God wants to live powerfully in, through, and for each generation of believers. He is the same yesterday, today, and forever. He is just as ready to manifest His mighty power today as at any time in the past.

Outline:

Verses 1-10 – Because of Israel's backsliding, they were given over to the Midianite oppressors who plundered their land of all its produce; however, God readily promised to deliver the people as soon as they cried to Him.

Verses 11-24 – The Angel of the Lord appeared to Gideon who was secretly threshing his grain. The angel's challenge to Gideon startled him because the young man envisioned himself as too weak and insignificant to make a difference. He also questioned the whole idea that God was still active on behalf of His people since he had not seen anything like the miracles of old occurring in contemporary history. When the angel caused his sacrifice to be consumed by supernatural fire, Gideon was convinced, and he named the place "The Lord is Peace," a prophetic declaration in a time of oppression.

Verses 25-32 – At the Lord's direction, Gideon recruited a team to help him destroy his father's pagan altar and build an altar to God on the same spot. When the men of the city discovered what had been done, they wanted to kill Gideon; however, his father intervened, saying that, if the pagan deity were really a god, he could judge the offender himself.

Verses 33-35 – Empowered by the Holy Spirit, Gideon called together an army to fight against the Midianites and the Amalekites.

Verses 36-40 – In order to remove all doubt that he was acting under God's supernatural direction, Gideon requested that the Lord perform two miracles as confirmation signs.

Prayer Focus: Lord, help me to see myself as a mighty man of valor for Your kingdom and to act promptly once I am certain that my directions are unquestionably from You. Amen.

Notes:

Spiritual Journal:

Week: Six
Day: Friday
Book: Judges
Chapter: Seven
Memory Verse: Two
Principle: Sometimes, we wind up in situations in which the odds are so impossibly against us that only divine intervention would rescue us. In these cases, we must remember that this is likely God's doing; He wants to show that it was indeed He who wrought the deliverance. He has declared that He will not share His glory with any man; therefore, He often brings His people through situations that could be solved only by Him.

Outline:
Verses 1-7 – God deliberately reduced the number of warriors with Gideon from over thirty-two thousand to just three hundred in order to ensure that the victory could never be claimed to have been the result of human military power.

Verses 8-14 – Gideon was given yet another supernatural sign that God was working through him when he slipped into the enemy camp and overheard the people talking about a dream which they interpreted as meaning that Gideon was to overpower their army.

Verses 15-25 – After Gideon's three hundred warriors routed the camp by blowing their trumpets, breaking the pitchers that concealed their torches, and shouting, the hosts of Israel pursued the enemy and reclaimed the land.

Prayer Focus: Lord, help me not to fear when I get to the end of my rope, because that is where Yours begins. Amen.

Notes:

Spiritual Journal:

Week: Seven
Day: Monday
Book: Judges
Chapter: Eight
Memory Verse: Thirty-five

Principle: This chapter illustrates the principle that Jesus taught us in the Golden Rule: that we should do unto others as we would have them do unto us.

Outline:

Verses 1-3 – The men of Ephraim were upset because they were not called into the initial assault by Gideon; however, they were allowed to assist in the continued pursuit of the enemy.

Verses 4-9 – Two different cities refused to provide food for Gideon's famished troops.

Verses 10-13 – Gideon defeated the remaining fifteen thousand Midianites (one hundred twenty thousand had already been killed) and captured their two kings.

Verses 14-17 – Gideon took revenge upon the two cities that had refused to assist his army.

Verses 18-21 – Because the Midianites had killed his relatives, Gideon declared that their kings must be executed. When his young son was unwilling to carry out the order, Gideon personally slew the rulers.

Verses 22-28 – Although Gideon refused to accept the people's proposal that he become their king, he did require a tribute from the people of Israel. He used his wealth to set up a memorial in his hometown. Unfortunately, the people used this memorial as a place of idolatry.

Verses 29-32 – Gideon lived to be an old man and had seventy sons through his many wives and at least one concubine.

Verses 33-35 – Israel did wickedly by not continuing to serve God or to show honor to the family of their liberator Gideon.

Prayer Focus: Lord, help me to always show kindness to those in need and respect to those who deserve honor. Amen.

Notes:

Spiritual Journal:

Week: Seven
Day: Tuesday
Book: Judges
Chapter: Nine
Memory Verses: Nineteen and twenty
Principle: The New Testament expresses today's thought in terms of sowing seed and reaping the resulting harvest: good seed yields a good harvest, and bad seed yields an evil harvest.
Outline:
Verses 1-6 – Abimelech, Gideon's son by the concubine, convinced the men of his home area to rise up against Gideon's legitimate heirs and slay them so that he could be declared king. As a result, all but one of Gideon's sons were slaughtered.

Verses 7-21 – Jotham, the one son who escaped assassination, proclaimed a judgment upon the people for their treachery by telling a parable about the trees' asking the thorn bush to be their ruler.

Verses 22-57 – As the prophetic judgment had proclaimed, Abimelech rose up against the men of Shechem and destroyed them; but, in the process, he received a fatal blow at the hand of a woman from Millo.

Prayer Focus: Lord, help me to always act in a way that guarantees a good harvest. Amen.
Notes:

Spiritual Journal:

Week: Seven
Day: Wednesday
Book: Judges
Chapter: Ten
Memory Verse: Sixteen
Principle: The Lord does not desire for His people to suffer; however, He must allow it occasionally when we are in rebellion against Him.
Outline:

       Verses 1-2 – Tola rose up as a deliverer and judge over Israel.

       Verses 3-5 – Jair followed as the next judge of the people.

       Verses 6-18 – When Israel again turned away from God to idolatry, they were again subjected to oppression by their enemies. Finally, the people cried out for deliverance, but the Lord was unwilling to rescue them until they showed true repentance for their dependence upon the pagan gods.

Prayer Focus: Lord, help me to never turn to You just as a means to get relief from my problems; rather, let me turn to You because I truly believe in You and want to serve You and live for You. Amen.

Notes:

Spiritual Journal:

Week: Seven
Day: Thursday
Book: Judges
Chapter: Eleven
Memory Verse: Thirty-five
Principle: We must carefully guard our words because we are obligated to honor them.
Outline:

> Verses 1-11 – In a time of distress, the people of Israel turned to Jephthah for help, even though he had been cast out years before because he was an illegitimate son. His requirement for agreeing to help was that he be accepted as ruler if he was able to led them to victory.

> Verses 12-28 – After negotiating with the enemy and recounting the wrongs that they had historically perpetrated against the people of Israel, Jephthah finally concluded that to attack was his only viable option.

> Verses 29-33 – Before entering into the conflict, Jephthah made a vow to sacrifice the first thing which came out to greet him when he returned successfully from the battle. Although it may seem honorable on the surface, this was a very foolish pledge because God had given a very specific list of animals that were acceptable for sacrifice and very specific conditions that these animals must meet in order to be acceptable. It was very likely that Jephthah was actually setting himself up to commit sacrilege by offering an unclean animal or even a clean animal that was blemished and therefore unacceptable.

> Verses 34-40 – Upon his return, Jephthah was greeted by his young daughter and was obligated to fulfill his vow by offering her as a sacrifice.

Prayer Focus: Lord, help me to carefully choose all my words so that they always honor You and to wisely guard my lips so that any obligation which I make will bless You. Amen.

Notes:

Spiritual Journal:

Week: Seven
Day: Friday
Book: Judges
Chapter: Twelve
Memory Verse: Three

Principle: Love and faith require action also. A poignant story is told of a Protestant leader in Germany during the Nazi era. He said that he did nothing when the Nazis came to take the Jews because he wasn't a Jew. He also did nothing when they came to take the Catholics because he wasn't a Catholic. Finally, when they came to take the Protestants, there was no one left to help. We are as – Cain discovered – our brother's keeper.

Outline:

Verses 1-7 – Conflict arose with the tribe of Ephraim because they did not assist in the battle against the army of Ammon. Jephthah's warriors picked out and killed the Ephraimites, who were easily distinguished by their accent.

Verses 8-15 – A series of judges including Ibzan, Elon, and Abdon ruled Israel for the next quarter century.

Prayer Focus: Lord, help me to never say I care without also proving it. When I fold my hands in prayer, may I also add my feet in action. Amen.

Notes:

Spiritual Journal:

Week: Eight
Day: Monday
Book: Judges
Chapter: Thirteen
Memory Verse: Twenty-three
Principle: We must always believe – as did Manoah's wife – that God is on our side, not against us. II Chronicles 16:9 teaches us that the eyes of the LORD run to and fro throughout the whole earth, looking for an opportunity to show Himself strong on the behalf of them whose heart is perfect toward Him. Jeremiah 29:11 further states that His intentions toward us are thoughts of peace, and not of evil, to give us an expected end.
Outline:
Verses 1-7 – After an angel appeared to Manoah's barren wife to announce that she was to bear a son who was to serve God through a special Nazarite vow, she rushed home to share the news with her husband.
Verses 8-14 – After Manoah prayed that the angel would reappear, he visited the wife a second time. This time, Manoah was nearby, so his wife brought him to meet the angel, who repeated the promise and instructions concerning the child.
Verses 15-21 – The angel manifested himself as a supernatural being by ascending to heaven in the flames of the sacrifice Manoah had offered to the Lord.
Verses 22-23 – Manoah responded fearfully at the miraculous manifestation; however, his wife responded in faith that God had good intentions toward them and their child.
Verses 24-25 – Their miracle child, Samson, was born and began to manifest the Spirit of God in his early years.
Prayer Focus: Lord, help me to have faith and always trust that You are always looking for opportunities to bring blessing into my life. Amen.
Notes:

Spiritual Journal:

Week: Eight

Day: Tuesday

Book: Judges

Chapter: Fourteen

Memory Verse: Six

Principle: Even the greatest of men have clay feet and are totally mortal, carnal, and fallible; the only thing that makes them "superhuman" is the anointing of the Holy Spirit of God.

Outline:

> Verses 1-4 – Against his parents' advice, Samson insisted that a marriage be arranged for him with a Philistine girl – one of Israel's enemies.

> Verses 5-9 – On the way to the betrothal, Samson slew a lion. When he returned for the wedding, he discovered that a colony of bees had built a nest and were producing honey inside the remains of the beast.

> Verses 10-18 – After joining in a wager with Samson that they could unravel his riddle, the Philistine men threatened his bride until she was forced to entice Samson to reveal his secret to her.

> Verses 19-20 – Under the anointing of the Spirit of God, Samson slew thirty Philistines and took their garments to pay off his wager. When he left the area, his new bride was married to one of the Philistine men in the wedding party instead of to Samson.

Prayer Focus: Lord, help me to continually live and walk in the Spirit so that I will not fulfill the lusts of the flesh, which are an ever-present danger. Amen.

Notes:

Spiritual Journal:

Week: Eight
Day: Wednesday
Book: Judges
Chapter: Fifteen
Memory Verse: Three
Principle: Even though the Bible teaches us to pursue peace with all men and to turn the other cheek when insulted or assaulted, it also teaches the necessity of justified conflict to stop aggression and abuse.
Outline:
Verses 1-5 – By releasing foxes with flaming torches tied to their tails into the wheat fields, Samson took revenge upon the Philistines for giving his bride to another man.

Verses 6-8 – When the Philistines retaliated by executing Samson's bride and father-in-law, he attacked and slaughtered a great number of them.

Verses 9-13 – After being threatened by the Philistines, three thousand Israelite men came to Samson and convinced him to surrender to the enemy.

Verses 14-19 – Under the anointing of the Holy Spirit, Samson broke free of the ropes which bound him, took hold of a piece of bone, and slew one thousand of the Philistine warriors. Following this victory, the Lord performed another miracle of provision by supplying a spring of water to refresh His servant.

Verse 20 – Samson ruled Israel for twenty years.

Prayer Focus: Lord, give me humility to submit to Your command of peace when You direct me not to avenge myself, wisdom to know when to use force to defend right, courage to follow through when force becomes necessary, and faith to trust You for victory when conflict occurs. Amen.
Notes:

Spiritual Journal:

Week: Eight
Day: Thursday
Book: Judges
Chapter: Sixteen
Memory Verse: Twenty

Principle: We must be careful of the relationships we allow ourselves to develop with the people, possessions, and philosophies of this present world system. They can easily seduce us from our intimacy with the Lord. Tragically, we often don't realize what affect these alien relationships are having until they have done great damage to our spiritual lives.

Outline:

Verses 1-3 – Samson had one illicit relationship but escaped unscathed. Perhaps this episode made him let down his guard and feel secure to enter into another ungodly friendship.

Verses 4-17 – Delilah continued to press Samson until he revealed his secret. It is surprising that he allowed himself to fall into her trap after having seen how he was tricked by his bride concerning the riddle and how Delilah had followed through with each of the false answers he offered her.

Verses 18-20 – When Delilah had his head shaved, Samson lost not only his strength but also his anointing. The saddest part of the story is that it happened without his even being aware of what was happening to him.

Verses 21-31 – Even though the Philistines won a great victory over Samson and made a public mockery of him, the Lord avenged the penitent judge and allowed him one last triumph in his moment of death.

Prayer Focus: Lord, help me to always be aware of the sins and weights which can so easily entangle and ensnare me. Amen.

Notes:

Spiritual Journal:

Week: Eight
Day: Friday
Book: Judges
Chapter: Seventeen
Memory Verse: Six
Principle: When we do not recognize God's set of absolutes as our standard for conduct, we tend to create our own flawed code of moral, social, and ethical standards.
Outline:

Verses 1-5 – In an intriguing story that reveals an utter lack of understanding of God's laws, Micah steals money from his own mother. She places a curse in the name of God upon the thief, and then Micah confesses that he is the culprit and receives a blessing from her – again in the name of God. In an even more surprising twist in the storyline, the mother reveals that she had dedicated the money to build two idols – a direct violation of the Ten Commandments.

Verse 6 – The root cause of such disobedience is revealed as being man's tendency to become his own standard and a law unto himself.

Verses 7-13 – Micah furthers his mother's error by hiring a Levite to serve as a priest in the idolatrous shrine in his home.

Prayer Focus: Lord, help me not to follow my own ways but to diligently seek after Your directions and standards in every area of my life. Amen.
Notes:

Spiritual Journal:

Week: Nine
Day: Monday
Book: Judges
Chapter: Eighteen
Memory Verse: Thirty-one
Principle: Just as Dan served idols while the rest of Israel worshiped God in the tabernacle, it is possible for us to harbor sinfulness in some areas of our lives while we honor God and do righteously in others. However, if we read on to the end of the Bible, we will see that those who nurture hidden sin are excluded from the kingdom of God just as the tribe of Dan is excluded in the listing of the tribes of Israel in Revelation.

Outline:
Verses 1-10 – When five spies from the tribe of Dan are sent to spy out a place for them to take as their inheritance, they happen upon the house of Micah and discover that he has a Levite serving as the priest in his household shrine.

Verses 11-26 – When the six hundred raiders from Dan head back to take the cities that the spies had chosen, they stopped at Micah's house, coerced the priest to serve them, and forcibly took the idols from Micah.

Verses 27-31 – When the Danites established themselves in Laish, they also established a place of idolatry which remained throughout their history.

Prayer Focus: Lord, just as I will not drink water that is 98% pure, containing only 2% sewage, I will not serve You with anything less than 100% of myself. Amen.

Notes:

Spiritual Journal:

Week: Nine
Day: Tuesday
Book: Judges
Chapter: Nineteen
Memory Verse: Thirty
Principle: Life is full of unusual and unexpected turns and twists; some of them are totally outside our control, while many of them are the results of our poor choices.
Outline:

Verses 1-3 – When the concubine of a certain Levite decided to leave him for a life of prostitution, the gentleman decided to follow her to her hometown and restore her to himself.

Verses 4-10 – In an apparent attempt to keep his daughter from returning with her husband, the girl's father continued to delay their departure until the Levite finally determined to leave against the father-in-law's will.

Verses 11-21 – In defiance of the custom of the day, no one in the city of Gibeah offered the travelers a place to stay until an old man from Ephraim, who was living in the city, brought them into his house.

Verses 22-26 – When a band of homosexual men attempted to assault the visitor, the host – in accordance with the then-current code of ethics concerning protecting one's guest – offered his virgin daughter to them instead. The men refused but finally accepted the Levite's concubine whom they molested all night long and returned to the doorstep at daybreak.

Verses 27-30 – When the Levite discovered that she was dead, he dissected her corpse and sent the pieces to the twelve tribes of Israel as a call to arms over the incident.

Prayer Focus: Lord, help me to make wise choices so as to prevent as many calamities as possible in my life and grant me Your wisdom to deal with all the misfortunes which come, whether self-induced by my poor choices or whether imposed by the hostile god of the present age. Amen.

Notes:

Spiritual Journal:

Week: Nine
Day: Wednesday
Book: Judges
Chapter: Twenty
Memory Verse: Fourteen
Principle: One great American leader once said that the only requirement for evil to prevail was that good men do nothing. Even more tragic is when men who are rather neutral – neither evil nor necessarily good – side with evil men because of political, relational, or financial reasons.
Outline:
        Verses 1-11 – When the people of Israel received the bloody message from the Levite, they rose in unity and determined to avenge his loss.
        Verses 12-16 – Rather than turning them over for prosecution, the men of the tribe of Benjamin decided to defend those guilty of this heinous crime.
        Verses 17-28 – After two days of heavy losses at the hands of the Benjamites, the people of Israel were assured by the priest of victory the following day.
        Verses 29-48 – By feigning defeat, the Israelites were able to draw the Benjamites into an ambush and totally overthrow them.
Prayer Focus: Lord, help me to always be able to clearly see right and wrong and to boldly stand up for what is right and never be blinded by peripheral circumstances that would draw me toward the wrong. Amen.
Notes:

Spiritual Journal:

Week: Nine
Day: Thursday
Book: Judges
Chapter: Twenty-one
Memory Verse: Six
Principle: Even if we are drawn into unavoidable conflict – or if we have entered into conflict that could have been avoided – we must be quick to heal the rifts created with those whom we have opposed.
Outline:
Verses 1-7 – The people of Israel lamented that the men of Benjamin would be left without wives and lose their inheritance because their wives had been killed in the invasion of their cities.

Verses 8-14 – Because the Israelites had made a declaration to destroy any tribe which did not assist in the attack against Benjamin, they attacked the one village which had not joined in the fight and took the virgin girls as wives for the men of Benjamin

Verses 15-23 – When they saw that there were not enough wives for all the men, the Israelites devised a plan in which the men of Benjamin were to abduct wives for themselves during the annual feast at Shiloh. This scheme was a way of allowing the men to marry daughters from the tribes of Israel yet leave the fathers of the girls technically innocent of violating the pledge that no one was to give his daughter in marriage to a Benjamite.

Verses 24-25 – These verses convey the most important message in this section of the book of Judges. Regarding all the unusual, unethical, and – frankly – bizarre events recorded in the concluding chapters of the book, the author explains that these actions were not necessarily right or acceptable to the Lord because the people at this time were without divine oversight and were doing what seemed right in their own eyes.

Prayer Focus: Lord, help me to always remember that, as Proverbs says, the way that seems right to my own human understanding is often the path which leads to destruction. I pray as Jesus taught me to pray that my steps would not be led into the way of temptation. Amen

Notes:

Spiritual Journal:

Week: Nine
Day: Friday
Book: Ruth
Chapter: One
Memory Verse: Sixteen
Principle: The most important decision we make in life is to accept Jesus Christ as Lord and Savior; the second most important decision goes along with it: choosing to associate with those who also serve Him.
Outline:
Verses 1-5 – A famine in the region of Bethlehem sent Naomi's family into Moab in their quest for survival; however, within a ten-year period, Naomi's husband and two sons all died in the land of Moab.

Verses 6-13 – The custom of the time provided for childless widows by requiring that the younger brother of the deceased should marry the widow. In Naomi's case, there were no younger sons to marry the widowed daughters-in-law and she was too old to have more children. In addition, it was impractical to expect the girls to wait and marry boys who would be so much younger than they. Therefore, she asked the girls to follow another custom of the time and return to their parents' homes and allow their fathers to make arrangements for them to remarry.

Verses 14-18 – One daughter-in-law agreed to the plan, but Ruth tenaciously clung to Naomi and pledged to convert to her religion and be naturalized to her nationality.

Verses 19-22 – Although Naomi's old acquaintances were happy to receive them when the two ladies returned to Bethlehem, Naomi returned with a sorrowful heart. Because of the losses she had experienced in Moab, she asked that her friends call her Mara, which means "bitterness," rather than Naomi, which means "pleasant."

Prayer Focus: Lord, I know that bad company corrupts good morals and that a man is known by his friends. Help me to tenaciously cling to You and to the righteous people You would have in my life. Amen.

Notes:

Spiritual Journal:

Week: Ten
Day: Monday
Book: Ruth
Chapter: Two
Memory Verse: Twelve
Principle: God does not make accounting mistakes; He carefully orchestrates the events of life to assure that each man reaps according to what he has sown. (Galatians 6:7)
Outline:
Verses 1-3 – Ruth humbled herself to work as a gleaner according to the custom of the day that provided for destitute people by allowing them to gather whatever was left in the fields after the hired workers had done their jobs.
Verses 4-17 – In her labors, she happened into the field of a relative of Naomi, who determined to show kindness to her for the kindness she had shown to her mother-in-law.
Verses 18-23 – Naomi immediately recognized that the events of Ruth's finding the field of Boaz and his showing favor toward her were the blessings of the Lord upon her and her daughter-in-law.
Prayer Focus: Lord, help me never to expect to reap Your benefits unless I'm also sowing blessings into the lives of others. Amen.
Notes:

Spiritual Journal:

Week: Ten
Day: Tuesday
Book: Ruth
Chapter: Three
Memory Verse: Eighteen
Principle: We need to be people of integrity who are so eager to always do what is right so that we have a sterling reputation among the people around us.
Outline:
Verses 1-9 – Naomi helped Ruth develop a plan to bring to Boaz's attention his legal responsibility to help the two women. Her visit to the threshing floor had none of the seductive sexual implications that may be read into it by modern readers. Lying at his feet was a way of communicating her dependence upon and submission to him. It is likely that this is the only way Ruth could have gotten to this busy, prominent member of the community, and it is also significant that she approached him at harvest time, the time of the year when he was the most secure financially.

Verses 10-13 – Boaz readily agreed to take responsibility for the two widows according to the custom that required that the closest living relative take responsibility for the property and dependents of a deceased family member. He, however, pointed out that one closer relative had to be approached first.

Verses 14-17 – Through the act of giving a generous supply of grain to the women, he demonstrated his good-faith promise to fulfill his obligation.

Verse 18 – Naomi expressed her confidence in Boaz's excellent character and sterling reputation.

Prayer Focus: Lord, help me to live as Jesus taught in the Sermon on the Mount so that people around me will see my good works and glorify You. Amen.
Notes:

Spiritual Journal:

Week: Ten
Day: Wednesday
Book: Ruth
Chapter: Four
Memory Verse: Fourteen
Principle: The original Greek version of Hebrews 13:5 contains a triple negative which could be literally translated to read, *I will not, no way, under any conditions ever leave or forsake you.*
Outline:

> Verses 1-10 – Boaz found the relative who was in line to redeem Naomi's property and offered him the chance. When the relative considered the fact that the deal included taking Ruth as his wife and fathering children through her to inherit Elimelech's estate, he declined the offer because he did not want to lessen the inheritance he was preparing for his own heir. In accordance with the custom of the time, he offered Boaz his shoe symbolizing that he was "walking away from the deal."

> Verses 11-12 – The elders of the city blessed Boaz for his generosity in redeeming Naomi's inheritance.

> Verses 13-17 – After a son was born to Ruth and Boaz, the women of the city blessed Naomi and the baby.

> Verses 18-22 – The ancestry of the baby is traced back to Perez, the son born to Judah and Tamar; his lineage is traced to King David.

Prayer Focus: Lord, help me to always believe and live by the line in the old song which says, "God will make a way where there seems to be no way." Amen.

Notes:

Spiritual Journal:

Week: Ten
Day: Thursday
Book: I Samuel
Chapter: One
Memory Verse: Seventeen
Principle: Hannah's life confirms the principles of James 5:16, which teaches us about getting results from God: *The effectual fervent prayer of a righteous man avails much.* She prayed effectively because her prayer was in line with the will of God; she prayed fervently because her prayer was an expression of the intensity of her desire, and she prayed righteously because her motivation was holy in that she was willing to give the baby to the Lord even though she had a strong maternal instinct to raise the child.

Outline:

Verses 1-7 – The ancient custom of sacrifice was that the pilgrimage to the tabernacle of the Lord was a time of family celebration as well as spiritual worship. The meat from the sacrificed animal was cooked and eaten at a joyous family reunion. However, the festivities were always marred in Elkanah's family because Peninnah ridiculed Hannah's childlessness.

Verses 8-18 – Hannah's deep anguish over her barrenness and the ridicule it brought her culminated in an intense prayer at the tabernacle, where the priest mistook her emotion for drunkenness. After she was able to explain herself and verbalize her request, the man of God prophesied that her prayer was to be granted.

Verses 19-28 – According to the timetable of nature, the Lord fulfilled His promise to Hannah and she, in turn, fulfilled her vow as soon as the child was weaned.

Prayer Focus: Lord, help me to extend my heart to You so that You can extend Your hand to me. Amen.

Notes:

Spiritual Journal:

Week: Ten
Day: Friday
Book: I Samuel
Chapter: Two
Memory Verse: Thirty
Principle: Promotion and position are not dependent upon ability or talent, but upon submission to and respect for the Lord.
Outline:

Verses 1-10 – Hannah sings a song of rejoicing, which accentuates the principle that God has exalted her because of her humility and submission to Him, while He has debased those who were arrogant and rebellious.

Verses 11-18 – The contrast between Samuel's holy service unto the Lord and the unrighteous way that Eli's sons abused their position as priests is emphasized by the double mention that Samuel *ministered before the Lord.*

Verses 19-21 – Hannah was blessed and further honored through the birth of more sons and daughters, proof that her barrenness had been reversed.

Verses 22-26 – In contrast to Eli's sons, who disregarded his attempts to correct their wickedness, Samuel grew in favor with both God and man.

Verses 27-36 – A man of God prophetically warned Eli that the Levitical family was going to suffer severe judgment from the Lord because of their arrogant sinfulness and Eli's lack of stern correction.

Prayer Focus: Lord, help me to humbly and willingly submit in Your service – not just so that I will be eligible for Your promotion but because I really desire to do what is pleasing in Your sight. Amen.

Notes:

Spiritual Journal:

Week: Eleven
Day: Monday
Book: I Samuel
Chapter: Three
Memory Verse: Ten

Principle: It was said of the financial advisor E. F. Hutton that when he spoke, people listened. Unfortunately, we too often fail to listen carefully to the Word of God.

Outline:

> Verses 1-8 – Three times, Samuel misunderstood the voice of the Lord for that of his mentor Eli.
>
> Verses 9-10 – After Eli realized that it was God speaking to Samuel, he instructed him how to respond properly when the Lord called him the next time.
>
> Verses 11-14 – The word that came from the Lord was confirmation of the prophecy of the man of God which spelled out judgment upon the house of Eli because of the sinfulness of his sons and Eli's failure to correct them.
>
> Verses 15-21 – Samuel's prophetic gift was confirmed by Eli and then by all the nation of Israel.

Prayer Focus: Lord, help me be like the sheep which Jesus spoke of who were able to recognize Your voice and would not follow any other. Let me be quick to hear You and to respond to Your voice. Amen.

Notes:

Spiritual Journal:

Week: Eleven

Day: Tuesday

Book: I Samuel

Chapter: Four

Memory Verse: Twenty-one

Principle: Rebellion and lack of regard for the Lord and His commandments result in His having to leave us to our own devices and destiny – without the glory of His presence and anointing.

Outline:

Verses 1-11 – When the Israelites realized that the Philistines were able to defeat them, they decided to bring the Ark of the Covenant to the battlefield, hoping that its presence would bring them the same victories the former generations had known under the leadership of Joshua. The result was exactly opposite from what they had hoped: the Philistines were frightened into an even more aggressive attack and defeated the Israelites. In the process, both of Eli's sons were killed and the Ark was captured.

Verses 12-18 – When the bad news reached the aged Eli, he was overwhelmed and, falling from his seat, died from a broken neck.

Verses 19-22 – When the news reached the pregnant wife of Phinehas, she went into labor and delivered a child whom she named Ichabod to signify that the glory of God had departed from Israel through the loss of the Ark. With this, she also died.

Prayer Focus: Lord, the Psalmist taught us that You inhabit the praises of Your people. Help me always to build a suitable dwelling place for You so that I will never lose the glory of Your presence. Amen.

Notes:

Spiritual Journal:

Week: Eleven
Day: Wednesday
Book: I Samuel
Chapter: Five
Memory Verse: Nine
Principle: The presence of God is a place of joy and blessing for those who are righteous before Him; for those who are wicked and rebellious before Him, God's presence brings judgment.
Outline:
Verses 1-5 – When the Ark was placed in the temple of the pagan god Dagon, the idol fell down and was broken into pieces. This symbolically depicted a spiritual conflict in which the God of Israel proved Himself more powerful than the pagan deity. An interesting note to this story is that when – more than three thousand years later – a film crew wanting to depict this incident went to Ashdod to photograph the ruins of the temple and get an exact depiction of the image of Dagon, they were told by the archeologists that no one had any idea of what the statue looked like!
Verses 6-10 – After the calamity at Ashdod, the Ark was sent to Gath, where its presence brought sickness and distress. Next, the Ark was relocated to Ekron where the death and suffering its presence invoked spurred the people to want to send it away.
Verses 11-12 – Because of the great anguish of the people, the lords of the Philistines decided to send the Ark back to the people of Israel.
Prayer Focus: Lord, when I think of the contrast between the anguish in the previous chapter (when the Ark was taken from Israel) and the anguish in this chapter (when the Ark was brought to the pagan Philistines), my heart cries out to always be the righteous person who treasures Your presence and is joyfully blessed in it. Amen.
Notes:

Spiritual Journal:

Week: Eleven
Day: Thursday
Book: I Samuel
Chapter: Six
Memory Verse: Twenty
Principle: It is a fearful thing to fall into the hands of the living God. (Hebrews 10:31)
Outline:

> Verses 1-9 – The spiritual leaders of the Philistines advised them to send the Ark back to Israel accompanied by golden gifts that represented the plagues inflicted upon them during the time the Ark was in their possession. In an attempt to prove whether the plagues were really from God or simply happenstance, they suggested that the Ark be sent away on a cart drawn by cows whose calves had been taken away and that the cows be allowed to choose their own course. If these beasts, which had not been trained to work as harnessed team animals, were to go directly to Israel, it would be a sure sign that the Ark belonged to the living God.
>
> Verses 10-12 – The experiment of the Philistines successfully proved the deity of the Lord.
>
> Verses 13-18 – The people of Beth Shemesh rejoiced to see the Ark and offered the cows which brought the Ark back to them as a burnt offering to the Lord.
>
> Verses 19-21 – However, tragedy in the form of the death of over fifty thousand men struck Beth Shemesh because they failed to observe the proper protocol concerning the Ark.

Prayer Focus: Lord, help me to never take Your presence lightly nor disregard Your anointing. Amen.

Notes:

Spiritual Journal:

Week: Eleven

Day: Friday

Book: I Samuel

Chapter: Seven

Memory Verse: Three

Principle: Our only hope for victory in life's circumstances is whole-hearted surrender to the Lord.

Outline:

       Verses 1-2 – The Ark was placed under the care of Eleazar, son of Abinadad, of Kirjathjearim.

       Verses 3-6 – Samuel called the people of Israel to repentance and gathered them at Mizpah to dedicate themselves to God.

       Verses 7-14 – The Philistines thought to take advantage of the fact that all Israel was gathered into one place and planned to attack them at Mizpah; however, Samuel interceded and God gave the Israelites victory, freeing them from the threat of Philistine encroachment.

       Verses 15-17 – Samuel headquartered himself at Ramah but traveled a circuit including Bethel, Gilgal, and Mizpah as he served as judge over Israel.

Prayer Focus: Lord, help me never to forget that my only key to victory in any area is to keep my heart totally unlocked before You. Amen.

Notes:

Spiritual Journal:

Week: Twelve
Day: Monday
Book: I Samuel
Chapter: Eight
Memory Verse: Seven
Principle: Disregard for divinely appointed authority is not resistance to human power but rebellion against God who placed that individual in power.
Outline:
> Verses 1-5 – When Samuel's dishonest sons were positioned to replace their godly father, the people of Israel requested that a king rather than a judge be placed in power over them.
>
> Verses 6-9 – When Samuel questioned the Lord concerning the request of the people, He responded that the people should be given what they requested. God honored the desire of the people even though it was against His will and it would wind up being hurtful to them. No mention is made of whether the Lord was pleased or not with the selection of Samuel's sons. It can only be assumed that He had intended to deal with the unqualified young men the same way he had dealt with Eli's wicked sons – remove and replace them, yet keep the system of having a judge rather than a king in leadership of the nation.
>
> Verses 10-18 – Samuel detailed the abuses that would be inflicted upon the people by the king once he was in power.
>
> Verses 19-22 – Nonetheless, when the people insisted that they be given a king like the neighboring nations, God instructed Samuel to do as they demanded.

Prayer Focus: Lord, help me to pray as Jesus did, *Not my will, but thine be done!* – even if it takes going through the agony which Jesus experienced in the Garden of Gethsemane to get to that place of brokenness and submissiveness. Amen.

Notes:

Spiritual Journal:

Week: Twelve
Day: Tuesday
Book: I Samuel
Chapter: Nine
Memory Verse: Nine
Principle: God never leaves His children in the dark. If we seek Him diligently, He will speak to us and give us insight beyond natural human wisdom. *Surely the Lord GOD will do nothing, but he revealeth his secret unto his servants the prophets.* (Amos 3:7) *He that hath an ear, let him hear what the Spirit saith unto the churches.* (Revelation 2:7)

Outline:

Verses 1-2 – Saul is introduced through recounting his lineage and declaring the exceptional height of his stature and his strikingly handsome features.

Verses 3-14 – A quest for his father's lost donkeys led Saul and his servant on an extensive search ending in the village where Samuel was to hold a feast. Following his servant's suggestion, Saul went to seek Samuel because of his supernatural insight.

Verses 15-20 – Samuel had received advance revelation of Saul's coming and greeted him with information concerning the donkeys and an invitation to the banquet, accompanied with a promise of a special message from God the following day.

Verse 21 – When Samuel began to speak to him about his place of leadership in Israel, Saul immediately responded with arguments concerning his family's smallness, apparently forgetting that he was head and shoulders taller than anyone else in Israel.

Verses 22-24 – Saul was placed in the position of honor at Samuel's banquet.

Verses 25-27 – Before Saul left to return to his father's house, Samuel spent some private time with him revealing God's special plan for the young man who was to soon become Israel's deliverer and first king.

Prayer Focus: Lord, help me to have ears to hear what You desire to say and eyes to see what You wish to reveal but, most of all, a heart that seeks to hear and see what You wish to communicate to me. Amen.

Notes:

Spiritual Journal:

Week: Twelve
Day: Wednesday
Book: I Samuel
Chapter: Ten
Memory Verse: Six
Principle: The anointing of God upon one's life makes all the difference in the world; someone once described it this way, "The anointing of God is to the believer what a phone booth was to Clark Kent."
Outline:

Verses 1-7 – Samuel gave Saul three signs to expect, which were to confirm the prophecies spoken over him. There was one sign for each area of his personality: a message of his father's concern for his soul, bread for his body, and prophetic anointing for his spirit.

Verses 8-13 – The three signs were fulfilled and people took note of the change that had occurred in Saul through this special anointing.

Verses 14-16 – Saul kept the prophet's words a secret.

Verses 17-26 – Samuel came to Mizpah to sacrifice and to announce the appointment of a king. When Saul's family was selected, the young man was not to be found. After he was discovered hiding behind the baggage, he was presented to the people. Most of the congregation acknowledged Saul as the new leader and began to observe the instructions that Samuel had laid out concerning the role of the subjects and that of the royalty.

Verse 27 – Although some rebels spoke evil against him and refused to honor him with a gift, Saul did not try to take any revenge upon them.

Prayer Focus: Lord, let it be said of me that I am a man with a "different spirit." Amen.
Notes:

Spiritual Journal:

Week: Twelve
Day: Thursday
Book: I Samuel
Chapter: Eleven
Memory Verse: Six
Principle: For the believer, there is always a source of inner strength coming from the Spirit of God inside him to meet and conquer any and every external challenge.
Outline:

Verses 1-3 – When the Ammonites challenged Jabesh Gilead and threatened to put out one eye of each of its inhabitants, the people begged for a reprieve.

Verses 4-9 – When Saul heard the news, the Spirit of God stirred him to action resulting in the amassing of an army thirty-three thousand strong. It is interesting to note that Saul also involved Samuel in the mandate, showing that the transition from the period of judges to the era of kings was not yet complete.

Verses 10-13 – The enemy was soundly defeated, and the people wanted to show their solidarity behind Saul by executing all who had resisted his appointment as king; however, Saul refused to allow this to happen.

Verses 14-15 – Samuel led the people in an official inauguration of Saul as king.

Prayer Focus: Lord, thank You for Your promise that Your Spirit will raise up a standard every time the enemy comes against us, even when it seems like a flood. Amen.
Notes:

Spiritual Journal:

Week: Twelve
Day: Friday
Book: I Samuel
Chapter: Twelve
Memory Verse: Twenty-two
Principle: Even though we fail the Lord, He does not forsake us. His discipline must be seen as correction, not rejection.
Outline:

Verses 1-5 – Samuel began his address at Saul's coronation with a defense of his own leadership of the nation.

Verses 6-12 – Next, he gave the people a brief overview of their nation's history, emphasizing the many times God had delivered the people even though they had rebelled against Him.

Verses 13-15 – He continued with the admonition that things would be the same under the leadership of a king: if the people rebel against God, they will be judged; but if they follow the Lord, they will be blessed.

Verses 16-19 – When Samuel sealed his address with the miraculous sign of calling for an unseasonable thunderstorm, the people begged him to pray for them because of their rebellious request for a king to rule them.

Verses 20-25 – Samuel's concluding warning against rebellion was wrapped in the encouragement that the people should continue to trust and serve the Lord because He does not intend to forsake them even though they have forsaken His plan.

Prayer Focus: Lord, help me to always be bold enough to run back to You even after I stray from Your care through rebellion. Amen.
Notes:

Spiritual Journal:

Week: Thirteen
Day: Monday
Book: I Samuel
Chapter: Thirteen
Memory Verse: Fourteen
Principle: The greatest desire in God's heart is to have a man who has a heart like His own. Such a man will be highly favored and blessed. Men who resist the heart of God will find that they can never be established securely.
Outline:
Verses 1-2 – After establishing his rule, Saul pared down his military forces to a minimal three thousand men.
Verses 3-5 – When a conflict arose with the Philistines, they amassed an overwhelmingly huge force against the tiny army of Saul.
Verses 6-7 – The people of Israel reacted with great fear and began to desert.
Verses 8-9 – After waiting seven days for Samuel to come and present a sacrifice unto the Lord, Saul decided that he should go ahead and make the offering before his total army broke ranks.
Verses 10-14 – Samuel arrived as the ceremony was being completed, and Saul tried to defend his actions; however, the prophet refused the king's explanation and declared that he had acted foolishly to presume upon the Lord as he had done. The judgment was that his kingdom, which would have been established as an ongoing dynasty, was going to be given to someone with a heart like God's own heart.
Verses 15-23 – Saul's conditions were desperate. By this point, his forces had dwindled to a mere six hundred men; the Philistines were amassed and were sending out sorties along three different fronts; and, worst of all, the Israelites had no weapons because the Philistines possessed the technology of ironworking and had only allowed the Israelites to have implements for farming.
Prayer Focus: Lord, help me to continually guard my heart, for it is the source of all the issues of life – both good and evil. Amen.
Notes:

Spiritual Journal:

Week: Thirteen
Day: Tuesday
Book: I Samuel
Chapter: Fourteen
Memory Verse: Six
Principle: The deciding ballot is always in God's hand – no matter if the number of voters on His side is small.
Outline:

Verses 1-14 – When Jonathan and his armor bearer went out to attack a garrison of Philistine soldiers, they received a sign indicating that they would be successful. Having entrapped the enemy in a very confined place, the two Israelites slaughtered the entire garrison of twenty Philistines.

Verses 15-23 – When the noise of the battle reached the Israeli encampment, Saul called roll and discovered that only Jonathan and his armor bearer were missing. After calling for the Ark and inquiring of the priest, Saul called for an attack. In the conflict, all the Israelites who had abandoned the army and those who had aligned themselves with the enemy were encouraged to join with Saul's army in the fight for freedom.

Verses 24-36 – Saul had called for a full-day fast; but Jonathan, who was not present when the decree was made, ate honey that he found in the forest. When the warriors saw him eat and heard his defense that it would have been better to go into battle with the strength of a good meal, they began to slaughter and eat the animals that they had captured from the Philistines. When Saul realized that they were eating meat from animals that had not been properly butchered, he called for the men to bring their animals to a central place where they could be slaughtered properly and the proper sacrifice could be made to the Lord.

Verses 37-45 – When Saul inquired as to who it was that had incited the people to the feeding frenzy and learned that his own son had been the catalyst, he determined to execute him; however, the people insisted that Jonathan be spared.

Verses 46-52 – Saul was established as ruler over Israel and continued to defeat the Philistines at every encounter.

Prayer Focus: Lord, help me to never underestimate the fact that You are on my side – or rather that I am on Your side. Amen.
Notes:

Spiritual Journal:

Week: Thirteen

Day: Wednesday

Book: I Samuel

Chapter: Fifteen

Memory Verse: Twenty-two

Principle: As the heavens are above the earth, so are God's thoughts and ways above the thoughts and ways of man; therefore, it is rebellion and foolishness to think that our plans are superior to His.

Outline:

Verses 1-9 – Under the direction of the Lord, Samuel instructed Saul to totally obliterate the Amalekites as judgment for the hostilities they had perpetrated upon the Israelites during their exodus from Egypt. Although he did destroy the city and its inhabitants, Saul allowed the warriors to save the king and the best of the possessions of the Amalekites.

Verses 10-23 – The Lord instructed Samuel that He was displeased with Saul because of his rebellion against His explicit instructions. Saul had also become infected with pride that was demonstrated by setting up a memorial to himself – a striking contrast to the way he had bashfully hidden himself on his coronation day. When Samuel confronted Saul over his wrongdoing, the king – like Adam, who blamed the woman whom God had given him – tried to blame the people and ultimately to put the fault on God, to whom the spoils were to be sacrificed. Samuel defined the king's sin and proclaimed his judgment.

Verses 24-35 – In his final public act of support for the king, Samuel slaughtered King Agag; then, he departed, never to visit or counsel Saul again.

Prayer Focus: Lord, help me to never lean upon my own understanding but to continually acknowledge Your direction in all my decisions. Amen.

Notes:

Spiritual Journal:

Week: Thirteen
Day: Thursday
Book: I Samuel
Chapter: Sixteen
Memory Verse: Fourteen
Principle: It is a very startling reality that we fall under the hand of judgment from the Lord as soon as we move out from His favor and blessing; there is no place of neutrality in the spiritual realm.
Outline:

Verses 1-5 – Several interesting points are revealed in this short section. First, we see that, even though Samuel had considered the appointment of a king to be a major error for the people of Israel, he actually mourned over Saul's fate; a true man of God does not let his personal opinion of who is at fault cloud his godly concern for each person's individual pain. Next, we see that Saul was willing to execute Samuel, the man who had been the greatest influence and blessing in his life; a man who does not have a heart truly after the heart of God will turn against even his closest friends – and, in fact, even against himself – when in a tight place. The men of Bethlehem were fearful at Samuel's arrival in their town; a true man of God will have the reputation of a bearer of God's correction as well as an avenue of His blessing.

Verses 6-13 – In reviewing the sons of Jesse to pick a king, Samuel was impressed by the physical appearance of David's older brothers, but God revealed to him that He was looking at the qualities of their hearts.

Verse 14 – This is a very troubling verse to any who read it to say that God commissioned an evil spirit to harass Saul; however, if viewed in light of a couple other biblical passages, it is easily understood. In the early chapters of Job, we see the devil standing before God, asking permission to torment righteous Job; only with God's permission did he depart to harass him. He went out from the Lord, but we could not say that he was actually commissioned by the Lord to do his diabolical deed. A similar story is told in the twenty-second chapter of I Kings where a lying spirit requested permission to deceive King Ahab. Again, he went out with the Lord's permission, but this verse should not be understood to mean that God initiated his errand.

Verses 15-23 – David was called to serve King Saul by calming him with music when the tormenting spirit harassed him. In that David was already recognized as a mighty man of valor and a man of war, it is likely that this section may actually be out of chronological order; it possibly follows after the battle with Goliath, which is recorded in the following chapter.

Prayer Focus: Lord, help me to live my life with the attitude of the line from that comical little Christian song which says, "I'm not cool, but that's okay; my God loves me any way." Help me to always remember – concerning others as well as myself – that it is what's on the inside, not the outside, that counts. Amen.
Notes & Spiritual Journal:

Week: Thirteen
Day: Friday
Book: I Samuel
Chapter: Seventeen
Memory Verse: Forty-five
Principle: The determining factor for success in life is neither brain nor brawn, but the blessing of God.
Outline:

Verses 1-16 – Goliath, the giant of Gath, kept the Israelite army paralyzed with fear for forty days with his threats and intimidation.

Verses 17-30 – David visited his brothers at the front line to bring supplies to them and news back to his father. While he was in the camp, he heard the challenge of the Philistine giant and the promise of reward from the king. David's response was entirely different from others present; he questioned the authority of the uncircumcised opponent to defy the army of God. Two major points show the uniqueness of David's perspective: he saw the giant as uncircumcised, meaning that he was not under a covenant with God as were the Israelites, and he saw himself as being part of the army of God Himself, whereas the other soldiers referred to themselves as *the army of Israel* or *the army of Saul*. David brought the whole matter into a divine perspective. When the others saw a big giant, David saw a bigger God. For him, this battle was of cosmic proportions.

Verses 31-39 – The lad was presented to the king, who was reluctant to allow him to accept the giant's challenge. However, the shepherd boy explained that he had proven the Lord's faithfulness in smaller – yet significantly dangerous – situations and was confident that the Lord would also bring victory in this one. After an unsuccessful attempt to dress the youth in the king's own armor (remember that Saul was almost a giant himself, being head and shoulders taller than all the rest of the men of Israel), Saul released David to go against Goliath.

Verses 40-44 – Goliath ridiculed David when he saw the youngster coming out to battle with a stick in his hand (likely a decoy to draw the giant's attention away from the real weapon he carried – the sling).

Verses 45-51 – Declaring that the battle was not to be determined by weaponry but by the authority of God Himself, David knocked the giant down with a blow from his sling and then decapitated him with his own sword.

Verses 52-54 – Encouraged by the defeat of the giant, the army of Israel (now seeing themselves as the army of the living God) slaughtered the enemy.

Verses 55-58 – David is recognized by the king as the hero of the day. Since this passage suggests that the king had not previously known David, it gives additional proof to the suggestion that chapters 16 and 17 may be out of chronological sequence.

Prayer Focus: Lord, help me always to remember that I can do all things through Christ who strengthens me. Amen
Notes & Spiritual Journal:

Week: Fourteen
Day: Monday
Book: I Samuel
Chapter: Eighteen
Memory Verse: Twelve
Principle: There should be an evident distinction between those who are filled with God's Spirit and those who are not; this distinction should be marked enough that those without the blessing of God upon their lives will recognize it and respect those who do walk under God's anointing.
Outline:
Verses 1-4 – Jonathan, the king's son, loved David and made a covenant with him. By giving David his robe, Jonathan was essentially offering him his place as heir to the throne; by giving him his weapons, he was essentially giving him his place as the recognized military hero of the nation.
Verses 5-29 – Saul became jealous of David because he could see that the young warrior was favored by God and honored by the people. In fits of madness and in calculated schemes of intrigue, Saul attempted to kill David. But in each case, David acted wisely and escaped.
Verse 30 – David continued to increase in his favor with the people and with God.
Prayer Focus: Lord, help me to always walk in that distinctly different place within Your favor – even when it may arouse envy, jealousy, or strife from those who do not share this blessing. Above all, grant me wisdom to properly appreciate the blessings and to graciously deal with the opposition. Amen.
Notes:

Spiritual Journal:

Week: Fourteen
Day: Tuesday
Book: I Samuel
Chapter: Nineteen
Memory Verse: Four
Principle: We must be cautious, as Gamaliel advised in Acts 5:39, that, in picking our opponents, we don't wind up fighting against God Himself.
Outline:
>
> Verses 1-8 – When Saul called all his servants together and directed them to find a way to kill David, Jonathan approached his father and counseled him that it would be sinful to execute David because he had done only good and not evil for Israel and the king.
>
> Verses 9-17 – After Saul, in another fit of rage, attempted to kill David, the king's daughter Mical rescued her husband by placing a statue in his bed and helping him escape through a window.
>
> Verses 18-24 – David sought refuge with Samuel. When Saul's henchmen came to arrest David, the Lord protected him by causing each of them, including Saul himself, to fall into ecstatic states of prophecy.

Prayer Focus: Lord, grant me enough wisdom to know how to fight for You, not against You. Amen.
Notes:

Spiritual Journal:

Week: Fourteen
Day: Wednesday
Book: I Samuel
Chapter: Twenty
Memory Verse: Seventeen
Principle: Even though blood may be thicker than water, there is also a friend that sticks closer than a brother. God-inspired love among the members of the Body of Christ is stronger than any natural relationship.
Outline:
> Verses 1-13 – Jonathan and David devised a plan whereby Jonathan could inform David of the king's intentions toward him.
>
> Verses 14-17 – Because of the sincere love between the two men, David made a covenant with Jonathan to always protect him and his family.
>
> Verses 18-34 – When Jonathan defended David for not attending the king's banquet, Saul became so enraged that he attempted to kill his own son.
>
> Verses 35-42 – Employing their secret code, Jonathan communicated to David the king's intent to kill him. After again renewing their commitment to each other, the two friends parted ways.

Prayer Focus: Lord, help me to always live with perfect love for and sincere commitment toward those whom You have placed in my life. Amen.
Notes:

Spiritual Journal:

Week: Fourteen
Day: Thursday
Book: I Samuel
Chapter: Twenty-one
Memory Verse: Eleven
Principle: Dr.Lester Sumrall said, "A banana tree doesn't need to wear a label saying *I'm a banana tree*; it just has to have bananas." When we bear the mark of God's destiny, the fruit of our lives will prove who we are without our having to tell anybody.

Outline:

Verses 1-6 – When David came to Ahimelech the priest and requested food, the only bread available was the shewbread which had been displayed before the Lord. Through a special concession, the bread was appropriated for David and his men to eat.

Verses 7-9 – David was also given the sword which had belonged to Goliath. This sword was very special because of its size and because it was made of iron when the rest of the Israelites had no iron implements of war.

Verses 10-14 – When David escaped to a Philistine city, the people there recognized the mark of destiny on him and would have killed him had he not feigned insanity to discredit the possibility that he would rise to greatness and become a threat to them.

Prayer Focus: Lord, help me live a life that shows forth Your hand upon it. Amen.
Notes:

Spiritual Journal:

Week: Fourteen
Day: Friday
Book: I Samuel
Chapter: Twenty-two
Memory Verse: Twenty-three
Principle: Even though our enemies may be formidable, God always provides a place of refuge and safety.
Outline:
Verses 1-2 – David's family and all the abused of Israel found refuge with David in the cave of Adullam.

Verses 3-5 – David arranged asylum for his parents in Moab while he and his men took shelter in a forest in Judah.

Verses 6-9 – When Saul accused his men of infidelity because they had not reported David's whereabouts to him, Doeg confessed to having seen him with the priest at Nob.

Verses 10-19 – After interrogating Ahimelech, the king ordered that he, along with eighty-five priests, be executed and the city of Nob be razed.

Verses 20-23 – The only son of Ahimelech who escaped the ravages of Saul found sanctuary with David and his men.

Prayer Focus: Lord, help me always to recognize the safe harbor You have provided, no matter what storms may rage. Amen.

Notes:

Spiritual Journal:

Week: Fifteen
Day: Monday
Book: I Samuel
Chapter: Twenty-three
Memory Verse: Two
Principle: The Lord has promised that He will hear and answer our cries unto Him – in fact, He has even promised to answer us even before we cry out – therefore, we must learn to call upon Him in every situation.

Outline:

Verses 1-6 – When David heard of a Philistine invasion, he promptly inquired of the Lord whether he should attempt to attack them. When his men feared to take up the challenge, David inquired a second time and received another positive response. After successfully delivering the city of Keilah, David and his men attempted to settle there.

Verses 7-15 – When Saul learned their whereabouts, he planned to ambush them in the city; however, David learned about his plot and inquired of the Lord what he should do. After the Lord warned him that the men of the city would betray him into the hand of the king, David and his men escaped. Saul, however, continued to pursue him into the wilderness.

Verses 16-18 – Jonathan found David and renewed his commitment to him and covenant with him even as Saul sought to kill him.

Verses 19-28 – The local residents revealed David's location to Saul, who surrounded him and was on the verge of capturing him when news of a Philistine invasion called him away.

Verse 29 – David escaped to En-gedi, a rugged oasis in the Dead Sea area.

Prayer Focus: Lord, teach me to always ask You for direction and to then listen expecting to hear Your answer; but, most of all, help me to always follow the instructions You give me. Amen.

Notes:

Spiritual Journal:

Week: Fifteen
Day: Tuesday
Book: I Samuel
Chapter: Twenty-four
Memory Verse: Twelve
Principle: God – not the offender or oppressed – is in charge of rectifying all injustices.
Outline:

> Verses 1-7 – When Saul entered into the cave where David was hiding, David had a perfect opportunity to kill the king; however, David refused because he considered Saul to be the anointed king regardless of the antagonism he was displaying toward David.

> Verses 8-15 – When they had left the cave, David confronted Saul with the corner of the robe he had secretly cut from the king's garment as evidence that he could have taken his life.

> Verses 16-22 – The king acknowledged David's loyalty and trustworthiness and confessed that he knew that David was destined to be king. He further requested that David pledge to preserve his family when he ascended to the throne.

Prayer Focus: Lord, grant me the nobility and humility it takes to allow You to avenge me rather than attempting to even the score myself. Amen.

Notes:

Spiritual Journal:

Week: Fifteen
Day: Wednesday
Book: I Samuel
Chapter: Twenty-five
Memory Verse: Thirty-three
Principle: Often, we need the wise advice of those who can see our situations from an outside perspective in order to protect us from our own plans which, in the long run, will harm us more than our opponents could.
Outline:
Verse 1 – Samuel died and was buried.
Verses 2-38 – When Nabal (whose name means "foolish") acted selfishly and unwisely by refusing to honor David's men who had served as protectors for his herdsmen and flocks in the wilderness, David determined to seek revenge upon him. When Nabal's wise wife Abigail brought provisions to David's troops and advised David not to take matters into his own hand, she seemed more concerned for the reputation of the future king than for the safety of her present husband. After David relented of his vengeance, Abigail returned to her husband and told him of how she had diverted the danger which he had brought upon himself. Nabal went into severe shock and eventually died because of the news his wife brought to him.
Verses 39-44 – David took Abigail as his wife along with Ahinoam while Saul gave his daughter Michal, David's first wife, to another man.
Prayer Focus: Lord, help me to always be open to the wisdom of those counselors You send into my life to protect me from evil and occasionally from myself. Amen.
Notes:

Spiritual Journal:

Week: Fifteen
Day: Thursday
Book: I Samuel
Chapter: Twenty-six
Memory Verse: Nine
Principle: We cannot attack God's people without incurring God's judgment.
Outline:

> Verses 1-12 – David had a second chance to take Saul's life, but he delivered him again, taking only his spear and water bottle as proof that he had the king in his hand.
>
> Verses 13-16 – David challenged Abner, Saul's military commander, for allowing the king to be left unprotected.
>
> Verses 17-25 – Again, Saul had to admit that he was acting wickedly and that David was operating in righteousness.

Prayer Focus: Lord, help me to consider others in the attitude with which You think of them. Amen.

Notes:

Spiritual Journal:

Week: Fifteen
Day: Friday
Book: I Samuel
Chapter: Twenty-seven
Memory Verse: One
Principle: Godly wisdom and common sense often coincide.
Outline:

>Verses 1-12 – While David hid from Saul for sixteen months by living among the Philistines, he raided the Canaanite cities but deceived the Philistines into thinking that he was raiding the villages of Israel.

Prayer Focus: Lord, help me to be both worldly wise and spiritually sensitive. Amen.
Notes:

Spiritual Journal:

Week: Sixteen

Day: Monday

Book: I Samuel

Chapter: Twenty-eight

Memory Verse: Six

Principle: When we refuse to listen to God's instructions, we may find ourselves so far outside His favor that we cannot hear from Him even when we desire to.

Outline:

Verses 1-2 – The Philistines recruited David to serve with them in their battles against Israel.

Verses 3-6 – Saul feared when he saw the armies arrayed against him, but he was unable to get a response from any of his inquiries of the Lord concerning how he should react to their attack.

Verses 7-19 – Even though he had outlawed mediums in the country, Saul turned to the witch of Endor in an attempt to consult with the dead prophet Samuel. When the prophet was called forth, he reprimanded Saul for his disobedience and warned him that he and his sons would die at the hand of the Philistines the following day and that David would eventually become king in his place.

Verses 20-25 – Saul was greatly traumatized by the message but was eventually convinced by the medium and his companions to have a meal and return to his battle station.

Prayer Focus: Lord, help me to always listen to Your voice and always stay in a close relationship with You so that I can always hear even Your faintest whisper. Amen.

Notes:

Spiritual Journal:

Week: Sixteen
Day: Tuesday
Book: I Samuel
Chapter: Twenty-nine
Memory Verse: Six
Principle: The favor of men is not important; God's favor is all that counts.
Outline:

> Verses 1-12 – David was asked to separate from the army of the Philistines for fear that he might turn traitor against them.

Prayer Focus: Lord, help me to always establish my self-worth based on Your opinion of me, not on that of men. Amen.
Notes:

Spiritual Journal:

Week: Sixteen
Day: Wednesday
Book: I Samuel
Chapter: Thirty
Memory Verse: Six
Principle: When everything around us is distressing and negative, we can still turn to God for strength and encouragement. Such a time of refreshing must be purposely self-initiated.
Outline:

Verses 1-8 – When David's men returned to their home base and discovered that the city had been raided and all the possessions as well as their wives and children had been taken, they turned against David and considered stoning him. When David turned to the Lord to ask if he should try to reclaim their losses, the Lord responded that he would be fully successful in the venture.

Verses 9-10 – Of David's six hundred warriors, two hundred were too exhausted to pursue the enemy so they stayed behind.

Verses 11-15 – An Egyptian servant of the marauders was able to lead David's men to their camp.

Verses 16-20 – When David attacked the invaders, he was able to recapture all the lost property and family members.

Verses 21-25 – Despite the protests of some of his men, David showed the true spirit of teamwork by dividing the spoils of the attack equally among all who had stayed behind and those who actually went into the battle.

Verses 26-31 – David also sent gifts from the plunder to the tribes of Israel.

Prayer Focus: Lord, help me to always run to You – not from You – in my times of trouble. Amen.

Notes:

Spiritual Journal:

Week: Sixteen
Day: Thursday
Book: I Samuel
Chapter: Thirty-one
Memory Verse: Four
Principle: A life lived in disrespect for God will end in a disrespectful death.
Outline:

        Verses 1-7 – Severely wounded in the battle, Saul begged his armor bearer to kill him; however, he refused. Saul ten took his own life. The armor bearer then followed in suicide and Saul's sons were also killed in the battle.

        Verses 8-13 – Saul's head and armor were taken by the Philistines as trophies for their temple, but brave men of Jabesh Gilead rescued his body for cremation and burial.

Prayer Focus: Lord, help me to live an honorable life so I can die a noble death. Amen.
Notes:

Spiritual Journal:

Week: Sixteen
Day: Friday
Book: II Samuel
Chapter: One
Memory Verse: Twenty-seven
Principle: All life – even the life of our oppressor – is precious and should be reverenced.
Outline:

> Verses 1-16 – When a messenger came to David purporting to have killed Saul, David and his men mourned the loss of the king and Jonathan; David had the messenger slain for having taken the life of God's anointed.
>
> Verses 17-27 – David composed a song of lament for the loss of Jonathan and Saul.

Prayer Focus: Lord, help me to have proper respect for the sanctity of life of all men, regardless of how they act toward me. Amen.

Notes:

Spiritual Journal:

Week: Seventeen
Day: Monday
Book: II Samuel
Chapter: Two
Memory Verse: Twenty-six
Principle: We must learn to put differences aside and put an end to senseless war.
Outline:

>Verses 1-7 – One of David's first acts after being proclaimed king in Hebron was to honor the brave men who buried the body of Saul.
>
>Verses 8-11 – Saul's son Ishbosheth was proclaimed king over Israel while David ruled Judah.
>
>Verses 12-32 – In a confrontation between the Israelite forces under Abner and the soldiers of Judah under Joab, Joab's brother pursued Abner and was slain. Only after Abner's plea that the conflict between the related people cease, did the opponents pull back and establish a truce.

Prayer Focus: Lord, help me to be a peacemaker who knows when and how to establish peace between brothers. Amen.

Notes:

Spiritual Journal:

Week: Seventeen
Day: Tuesday
Book: II Samuel
Chapter: Three
Memory Verse: Thirty-nine
Principle: The old expression, "What goes around comes around," sums up the effect of today's truth but fails to explain that the immediate cause of such recompense is the hand of God.
Outline:
    Verses 1-5 – As David and Ishbosheth continued at war, David gained in strength in military power and began to establish his house through the births of several sons.
    Verses 6-11 – Having been falsely accused by Ishbosheth, Abner retaliated by aligning himself with David and began to work to turn the loyalty of the people of Israel to him.
    Verses 12-16 – David demanded that Michal be returned to him as a sign that Abner was sincere in his shift in loyalties.
    Verses 17-21 – Once Abner had begun to win the favor of the people over to David, he made a personal visit to see him in Hebron.
    Verses 22-27 – Joab used this visit as an occasion to avenge the death of his brother Asahel by murdering Abner during a private meeting with him.
    Verses 28-39 – David mourned Abner's death and made a public declaration that he was not involved in the plot to take his life. In fact, he fasted so extensively that the people around him pleaded with him to take food. In addition, he placed a curse upon the descendants of Joab for this crime.
Prayer Focus: Lord, help me to always remember Your promise that vengeance is Yours and that You will repay; therefore, I don't have to get even when injustice is done to me. Amen.
Notes:

Spiritual Journal:

Week: Seventeen
Day: Wednesday
Book: II Samuel
Chapter: Four
Memory Verse: Eleven
Principle: Good results cannot be accomplished through evil acts. Even though they may be done in order to achieve a good purpose, wrong actions must never go unpunished.
Outline:

Verses 1-3 – Discouragement and uneasiness pervaded Israel after Abner's death.

Verse 4 – The story is recalled of how Jonathan's son Mephibosheth, as a five-year-old child, was crippled.

Verses 5-7 – Rechab and Baanah assassinate King Ishbosheth.

Verses 8-12 – When they present the head of the slain king to David, he has them executed for their evil act of murdering a righteous man.

Prayer Focus: Lord, help me to always judge my own motives and actions so I need not be judged for or by them. Amen.

Notes:

Spiritual Journal:

Week: Seventeen

Day: Thursday

Book: II Samuel

Chapter: Five

Memory Verse: Nineteen

Principle: The first and most important key to successful living is to ask the Lord's direction in each decision.

Outline:

        Verses 1-5 – The leaders of Israel recognized the fact that David had been anointed by God to be their king, and they covenanted their loyalty to him. He ruled for forty years – seven over Judah and thirty-three over all Israel.

        Verses 6-16 – David established his capital in Jerusalem. The city itself had never been conquered even though their army was one of the first defeated when Joshua entered the land. The city was so well defended by its location with deep ravines surrounding it, the Jebusites used only their blind and lame men to guard Jerusalem. David's army slipped in through the water system and took the city from inside. Once established in the city, David began to build a palace for himself with gifts received from Tyre, a neighboring kingdom. He also fathered a number of children there.

        Verses 17-25 – When the Philistines contested him, David always sought the Lord's direction before answering their challenge. The result was that God gave him a winning strategy each time.

Prayer Focus: Lord, help me to always remember that my ideas and schemes are never up to the same level as the plans You desire to give me. Amen.

Notes:

Spiritual Journal:

Week: Seventeen
Day: Friday
Book: II Samuel
Chapter: Six
Memory Verse: Twenty-two
Principle: We must determine that we will not be intimidated by other people's opinions of us; the only opinion that counts is God's.
Outline:

Verses 1-9 – When David decided to bring the Ark of the Covenant to Jerusalem, he did so without the proper reverence described in the books of Moses. The result was the death of one of the sons of Abinadab.

Verses 10-15 – After determining that the Ark was to be carried on the shoulders of men rather than on an ox cart, David arranged to have the holy symbol brought to Jerusalem in great pageantry with much rejoicing and abundant sacrifices.

Verses 16-19 – The gala celebration at the entry of the Ark into the city was commemorated with a distribution of gifts to the entire citizenry.

Verses 20-23 – When Michal criticized David for his emotional display at the celebration, he responded that he was willing to be even more humbled in the sight of men so that his praise would be acceptable unto the Lord. As a judgment for her critical attitude, Michal suffered barrenness for the rest of her life.

Prayer Focus: Lord, help me always to remember the simple rule for living enunciated by the late Dr.Lester Sumrall, "Another person's head is a very funny place for me to keep my happiness." Amen.

Notes:

Spiritual Journal:

Week: Eighteen
Day: Monday
Book: II Samuel
Chapter: Seven
Memory Verse: Twenty-one
Principle: God is a great God who does wondrous things and establishes great blessing in the lives of His people simply because it is His nature to do good.
Outline:

Verses 1-11 – When David told Nathan that he had decided that he wanted to build a Temple for the Ark of the Covenant, the prophet encouraged him to go ahead with his plan; however, the Lord later spoke to the prophet and directed him to tell David that it was not His will that David build a house (building) for God, rather God will build a house (dynasty) for David.

Verses 12-17 – God established an eternal covenant with David's family that a descendant of David's would always reign from the throne in Jerusalem.

Verses 18-29 – In humble gratitude, David expressed his praise to God who, simply to demonstrate His magnanimous nature, willingly lavishes unsolicited blessing on those who serve Him.

Prayer Focus: Lord, thank You that You have chosen me as a target for Your mercy and blessings. Amen.

Notes:

Spiritual Journal:

Week: Eighteen

Day: Tuesday

Book: II Samuel

Chapter: Eight

Memory Verse: Fifteen

Principle: Authority must be accompanied by equitable treatment of the subjects if it is to be righteous leadership.

Outline:

        Verses 1-14 – David continued to battle and conquer the surrounding enemies in order to establish the security of his own kingdom and the visible dominance of the kingdom of God.

        Verses 15-18 – David established a strong infrastructure of leadership inside the nation of Israel.

Prayer Focus: Lord, as You open opportunity for me to serve in any leadership positions, also help me to develop the godly character to qualify for that role. Amen.

Notes:

Spiritual Journal:

Week: Eighteen

Day: Wednesday

Book: II Samuel

Chapter: Nine

Memory Verse: Three

Principle: In serving as God's representatives in this world, showing forth the character of God through kindness is as important, if not more so, as demonstrating His authority.

Outline:

Verses 1-13 – David sought for and found Mephibosheth, the son of Jonathan, in order to deliberately bless him. When he was found, all his property was restored, servants were appointed to care for his estate, and daily provision was made for him and his family at the royal table.

Prayer Focus: Lord, help me to follow after the model which the scriptures set when they describe You as continually looking for opportunity to bless those who are in covenant with You. Amen.

Notes:

Spiritual Journal:

Week: Eighteen
Day: Thursday
Book: II Samuel
Chapter: Ten
Memory Verse: Two
Principle: We must always initiate kindness – even if it is not received.
Outline:

> Verses 1-5 – Hanun took David's act of condolence at his father's death as an act of aggression and used it as an occasion to abuse David's messengers.
>
> Verses 6-14 – Realizing that they had acted foolishly against Israel, the people of Ammon hired the Syrian army to assist them in confronting David's forces. Although they were outnumbered, the army of Israel divided and fought the enemy on two fronts, roundly defeating them on both.
>
> Verses 15-19 – Following the defeat of their mercenaries, the Syrians prepared to attack Israel. Again, the army of David soundly defeated them and brought them into subjection to Israel.

Prayer Focus: Lord, help me to show forth kindness just as You always do – even when I know that my kindness will only be spurned just as Your kindness is rejected so often. Amen.

Notes:

Spiritual Journal:

Week: Eighteen
Day: Friday
Book: II Samuel
Chapter: Eleven
Memory Verse: Twenty-seven
Principle: Even though we may be able to conceal our acts and motives from men and even win their favor, the really important issue in life is whether our actions please God.
Outline:
Verses 1-5 – David drew Bathsheba into an illicit affair that resulted in an illegitimate pregnancy.
Verses 6-13 – In an attempt to conceal his sin with Bathsheba, David called her husband home from the battlefront in hopes that it could be made to look as if the pregnancy were legitimate; however, the plan was spoiled because Uriah was too noble to allow himself to enjoy the pleasures of home while his comrades continued in battle.
Verses 14-25 – In a diabolical attempt to cover up the sin, David plotted to eliminate Uriah and set in motion a scheme that made it appear that his death was a wartime causality.
Verses 26-27 – Following a period of mourning for her husband's death, Bathsheba became the bride of the king.
Prayer Focus: Lord, help me to always live aware that Your all-seeing eye never fails to search out my actions and motives and that Your ever-sensitive Spirit is judging their worth. Amen.
Notes:

Spiritual Journal:

Week: Nineteen

Day: Monday

Book: II Samuel

Chapter: Twelve

Memory Verse: Thirteen

Principle: The only way to deal with sin is to first expose it to the light of God's conviction through the Holy Spirit and then cover it beneath the blood of God's Son, Jesus.

Outline:

Verses 1-7 – The prophet Nathan confronted David's sin through telling him a parable that exposed the nature of the king's wickedness.

Verses 8-12 – Judgment was declared against David's reign because of his sin.

Verses 13-14 – Even though David repented and was forgiven, certain punishments were still to be incurred.

Verses 15-23 – Even though David interceded with fasting, the illegitimate child's life was not spared.

Verses 24-25 – After mourning the death of the baby, David and Bathsheba were given another baby – Solomon – who was favored of God.

Verses 26-31 – Finally, the city of Rabbah, against which Uriah had fought, was conquered.

Prayer Focus: Lord, help me to have the courage and faith to confront my errors and sins and to deal with them honestly and confidently before You. Amen.

Notes:

Spiritual Journal:

Week: Nineteen
Day: Tuesday
Book: II Samuel
Chapter: Thirteen
Memory Verse: Twenty-one
Principle: David failed in his responsibility as a father because he became angry at the actions of his sons but did not take action to correct them.
Outline:
Verses 1-20 – David's son Amnon devised a plan by which he was able to molest his half-sister Tamar.
Verses 21-22 – Although David was upset at his son's sin, he did nothing either to correct the errant son or to restore the injured daughter. At the same time, there was a division between Amnon and Tamar's full brother Absalom. Again, David allowed this volatile situation to go unchecked.
Verses 23-33 – Absalom eventually took revenge upon Amnon and had him murdered. Another fault of David's parental abilities is demonstrated here in that he failed to see the warning signs when Absalom suddenly insisted that Amnon – after two years of estrangement – be his guest at the feast.
Verses 34-39 – Absalom's three-year exile also points to David's failure as a father when he did nothing to punish or restore his son.
Prayer Focus: Lord, help me to always remember that You have given me children as arrows in my hand so that I can direct their flight properly. Help me to properly fulfill this grave responsibility. Amen.
Notes:

Spiritual Journal:

Week: Nineteen
Day: Wednesday
Book: II Samuel
Chapter: Fourteen
Memory Verse: Thirteen
Principle: Separation between parents and their children is not simply a family matter; it is an obstruction of God's divine order.
Outline:
> Verses 1-24 – It took a plot by David's top general to arrange for Absalom to be returned to the city of David; however, he was still banished from his father's presence.
>
> Verses 25-33 – After two years of isolation, Absalom insisted that Joab arrange for him to be reunited with his father. It is apparent that the issue of Tamar's humiliation remained unresolved in Absalom's heart when he named his own daughter after his disgraced sister.

Prayer Focus: Lord, help me to learn to get over offenses and to bring healing rather than to allow injuries to continue to fester. Amen.
Notes:

Spiritual Journal:

Week: Nineteen
Day: Thursday
Book: II Samuel
Chapter: Fifteen
Memory Verse: Six
Principle: Subtlety and seduction are the most treasonous forms of anarchy.
Outline:

       Verses 1-12 – After undermining his father's position by winning the favor of the common citizens, Absalom retreated to Hebron and had himself declared king.

       Verses 13-23 – With great lament, David abandoned the city of Jerusalem.

       Verses 24-37 – In his escape, the king left behind men who were to infiltrate the insurgent regime, provide Absalom with unwise counsel, and then inform David of the plans of his son.

Prayer Focus: Lord, help me to have the wisdom of God to never be trapped by the subtlety and seduction of the enemy of my soul. Amen.

Notes:

Spiritual Journal:

Week: Nineteen

Day: Friday

Book: II Samuel

Chapter: Sixteen

Memory Verse: Twelve

Principle: God's opinion, not that of any man, is what determines our worth and our future.

Outline:

Verses 1-4 – Even though he had been favored by the king, Mephibosheth took David's misfortune as an occasion to try to profit at the king's expense.

Verses 5-14 – When Shimei accosted David, the king graciously ignored his insults – choosing to wait for God to determine his outcome.

Verses 15-19 – Hushai, whom David had planted in Jerusalem to bring confusion to Absalom's counsel, was successful in winning the insurgents' confidence.

Verses 20-22 – Ahithophel advised Absalom to show disrespect for his father by having open intercourse with his concubines. It is likely that this was Ahithophel's way of avenging the illicit relationship David had had with his granddaughter Bathsheba.

Prayer Focus: Lord, help me to always remember and live by the advice of the great teacher, Dr. Lester Sumrall, who said that another person's head is a very funny place for a person to keep his happiness. Amen.

Notes:

Spiritual Journal:

Week: Twenty
Day: Monday
Book: II Samuel
Chapter: Seventeen
Memory Verse: Fourteen
Principle: Our success or failure often lies in the advice we follow.
Outline:

        Verses 1-4 – Ahithophel gave Absalom wise counsel concerning pursuing his father and his army.

        Verses 5-14 – Although Hushai's advice had a certain authoritative tone to it, it was, in fact, a ploy to allow David time to establish himself securely and ready himself for the coming conflict. It was because God Himself was against Absalom that he followed the unwise counsel.

        Verses 15-22 – Through a careful chain of underground informants, intelligence of Absalom's plans was passed to David so that he could secure himself before the attack.

        Verse 23 – Insulted because his advice was rejected, Ahithophel committed suicide.

        Verses 24-26 – In his pursuit of David, Absalom appointed Amasa as head of his army. This choice seems to have been based on a standing personal conflict between Amasa and Joab who was leading David's forces.

        Verses 27-29 – David found support among the local people as he entrenched himself.

Prayer Focus: Lord, help me to know the difference between the wisdom which comes from above and the earthly wisdom which You have described in the book of James, *This wisdom descends not from above, but is earthly, sensual, devilish. For where envying and strife is, there is confusion and every evil work. But the wisdom that is from above is first pure, then peaceable, gentle, and easy to be entreated, full of mercy and good fruits, without partiality, and without hypocrisy.* Amen.

Notes:

Spiritual Journal:

Week: Twenty
Day: Tuesday
Book: II Samuel
Chapter: Eighteen
Memory Verse: Thirty-three
Principle: There is a family love that cannot be silenced even in deadly conflict.
Outline:

Verses 1-18 – Absalom's army was overpowered by David's forces and by the difficult terrain in which they had to fight. Absalom himself was entangled by the limbs of a tree and left vulnerable for attack by David's men. The first soldier who saw him refused to slay him because he was the king's son, even though he was also the king's enemy. Joab and his armor bearers killed Absalom and buried him in the woods that had swallowed him and his forces.

Verses 19-32 – When messengers were sent to bring the news to the king, Joab exercised discretion in not allowing a friend of David's family to bring the word because he knew that the news would be bitter even though it was a proclamation of the victory.

Verse 33 – David lamented bitterly over the death of his son.

Prayer Focus: Lord, help me to always keep a tender heart of love for all my family even if they turn against me and act like enemies. Amen.

Notes:

Spiritual Journal:

Week: Twenty
Day: Wednesday
Book: II Samuel
Chapter: Nineteen
Memory Verse: Twenty-two
Principle: There is no wisdom in using victory as an occasion to avenge oneself against those who have been in opposition.
Outline:

> Verses 1-8 – Joab had to convince David that his remorse over Absalom's death was demoralizing for the nation.
>
> Verses 9-14 – At the prompting of the king, the priests Abiathar and Zadok, led a movement of the people inviting David's return to Jerusalem.
>
> Verses 15-18 – A welcoming party arranged by Shimei ushered David and his household across the Jordan.
>
> Verses 19-23 – David prudently opted not to execute Shimei even though he had insulted and accosted him as he fled before Absalom.
>
> Verses 24-30 – Mephibosheth accused his servant Ziba of having deceived him at the time of David's evacuation from the royal city.
>
> Verses 31-39 – David honored the aged Barzillai by allowing him to remain in his home area.
>
> Verses 40-43 – David's popularity was so extensive that the tribes actually began to argue among themselves as to which should have the favor of being able to have the closest relationship with the king.

Prayer Focus: Lord, help me to demonstrate wisdom, kindness, and lenient tolerance when dealing with those who have opposed me. Amen.

Notes:

Spiritual Journal:

Week: Twenty
Day: Thursday
Book: II Samuel
Chapter: Twenty
Memory Verse: Nineteen
Principle: Justice must be meted out for wrongdoing; however, mercy must prevail lest the judgment also unnecessarily destroy the innocent.
Outline:

> Verses 1-5 – David used the rebellion of Sheba as an occasion to test the loyalty of Amasa, who had served under his son Absalom during his rebellion.
>
> Verses 6-7 – When it seemed obvious that Amasa was not truly on the side of the king, David sent Abishai and Joab to rally the forces.
>
> Verses 8-13 – After the assassination of Amasa, his forces reluctantly submitted to the leadership of David's captains.
>
> Verses 14-22 – With Sheba holed up in Abel of Beth, David's forces were determined to destroy the city; however, a wise woman of the city negotiated to save the city by arranging to have the rebel leader killed and his head delivered to Joab.
>
> Verses 23-25 – David's government was restored with loyal men in places of responsibility.

Prayer Focus: Lord, help me to act in wisdom, seeing the big picture of all the ultimate consequences of each of my actions rather than just looking for immediate solutions to present situations. Amen.
Notes:

Spiritual Journal:

Week: Twenty
Day: Friday
Book: II Samuel
Chapter: Twenty-one
Memory Verse: Fourteen
Principle: In this story's enigmatic mix of honor and dishonor, we learn that God respects vows of faith even when those who made them may be less than perfect in their scruples.
Outline:
>　Verses 1-2 – When Israel suffered under an extensive famine, David discovered that the cause was Saul's violation of the covenant that Joshua had made with the Gibeonites, who deceived him into proclaiming them as a protected people.
>
>　Verses 3-9 – As restitution for Saul's aggression against the Gibeonites, seven of his descendants were executed.
>
>　Verses 10-14 – After a great display of lament by the mother of two of the executed men, David ordered that these men, along with Saul and Jonathan, be given an honorable burial without respect for the dishonor of their lives or deaths.
>
>　Verses 15-22 – In a series of conflicts with the Philistines, all four of Goliath's brothers were killed by mighty men of David's forces.

Prayer Focus: Lord, help me to learn to see the good as well as the evil in others and to learn to treat others justly even when they don't seem to deserve it. Amen.
Notes:

Spiritual Journal:

Week: Twenty-one
Day: Monday
Book: II Samuel
Chapter: Twenty-two
Memory Verse: Two
Principle: The Lord deserves praise because He is the only source of victory.
Outline:

> Verses 1-51 – David composed an eloquent song of praise to the Lord extolling His deliverance and protection of David. The song highlights the miraculous way God has honored David's sincerity before Him and established him as the leader of the people. In this song, David acknowledges that it is only through the mercies of God that he has not been destroyed.

Prayer Focus: Lord, I praise You because You have demonstrated undeserved favor toward me. Amen.

Notes:

Spiritual Journal:

Week: Twenty-one

Day: Tuesday

Book: II Samuel

Chapter: Twenty-three

Memory Verse: Three

Principle: Tenderness along with strength, and justice along with righteousness, are necessary in order to be a godly leader.

Outline:

Verses 1-7 – David summed up his life in a poetic statement declaring that God had exalted him to the position he held and had given him the talents he possessed. He summarized his reign by saying that God had showed him the qualities necessary to be a godly leader and that, even though his house was not perfect, it had been blessed by God with an everlasting covenant which God had promised to secure. Ruling in the fear of the Lord required him not only to shine like the sun and refresh like the rain when dealing with God's people but also to burn like fire when dealing with rebellion.

Verses 8-39 – In the description of the thirty mighty men in David's personal elite forces, one particular story is told of how these men risked their lives simply to bring David a refreshing drink of water which he refused to drink, offering it instead as an oblation to God.

Prayer Focus: Lord, help me to demonstrate godly qualities of leadership in any area where I am given the opportunity to lead others. Amen.

Notes:

Spiritual Journal:

Week: Twenty-one
Day: Wednesday
Book: II Samuel
Chapter: Twenty-four
Memory Verse: Twenty-four
Principle: Although God desires obedience above sacrifice, He does respect our sacrificial gifts to Him.
Outline:

Verses 1-9 – David called for a census of the army – a direct negation of his faith statement in Psalm 20:7 where he said that his faith was not in his army but in the name of his God. Even though the general of his forces tried to dissuade him, the king was insistent that the poll be taken.

Verses 10-15 – In His great mercy, God gave David the opportunity to choose the judgment for his sin: seven years of famine, three months of conquest by the enemy, or three days of plague. Preferring to fall into the hand of God rather than the hand of man, David chose the plague.

Verses 16-17 – When the plague threatened the city of Jerusalem, David desperately repented and sought God's mercy.

Verses 18-25 – Following the counsel of the prophet Gad, the king went to the mountain top, which later became the site of the Temple, to offer a sacrifice. David refused the offer of the piece of ground for free, stating that he knew that he had to show his personal involvement by paying a personal price when sacrificing to the Lord.

Prayer Focus: Lord, help me to never take the easy way out – either by avoiding necessary sacrifice or by trying to substitute sacrifice for true obedience. Amen.

Notes:

Spiritual Journal:

Week: Twenty-one
Day: Thursday
Book: I Kings
Chapter: One
Memory Verse: Six
Principle: Failing to plan is planning to fail. Because David never gave clear instructions concerning which of his heirs was to succeed him, he set the stage for conflict between his sons.
Outline:
Verses 1-4 – In his old age, David was given Abishag the Shunammite woman, an especially beautiful nursemaid, to care for him.
Verses 5-10 – Adonijah collected supporters around himself and made the proclamation that he was going to ascend to the throne.
Verses 11-27 – Nathan and Bathsheba approached King David concerning his desire that Solomon should succeed him.
Verses 28-40 – David arranged for Solomon to be crowned to rule in his place.
Verses 41-53 – Adonijah feared for his life when he heard that Solomon had been crowned.
Prayer Focus: Lord, help me to always have the wisdom to plan for the future and the humility to allow You to direct those plans. Amen.
Notes:

Spiritual Journal:

Week: Twenty-one
Day: Friday
Book: I Kings
Chapter: Two
Memory Verse: Three
Principle: A father should invest his entire life into his son and not do as David did when he waited until the waning minutes of his life to give instruction to Solomon.
Outline:

Verses 1-9 – David gave Solomon last-minute advice and instruction.

Verses 10-12 – At David's death, Solomon ascended to the throne.

Verses 13-46 – Solomon's establishment on the throne bore marks of violence and bloodshed as he "cleaned house" of those who were possible threats to his security.

Prayer Focus: Lord, help me to see those teachable moments which occur daily and use them to impart something into the lives of those I am called to train and mentor. Amen.

Notes:

Spiritual Journal:

Week: Twenty-two
Day: Monday
Book: I Kings
Chapter: Three
Memory Verse: Nine
Principle: As Solomon later wrote in the book of Proverbs, wisdom is the principle thing because by it we can obtain prosperity and all the other benefits in life.
Outline:

Verses 1-15 – When Solomon dedicated his administration to the Lord by asking for wisdom to properly fulfill his role of leadership, the Lord answered by promising to grant his request and add to him all the material blessings which he bypassed in order to request wisdom.

Verses 16-28 – One of the first tests of Solomon's wisdom came when two prostitutes came to him with a living baby and the corpse of a dead baby. When each woman claimed to be the mother of the living baby, the king was able to discern the true mother by ordering that the baby be cut in half and shared by both.

Prayer Focus: Lord, help me to be wise enough not to pursue temporal blessings when You are offering the source of all blessings. Amen.

Notes:

Spiritual Journal:

Week: Twenty-two

Day: Tuesday

Book: I Kings

Chapter: Four

Memory Verse: Twenty-nine

Principle: Godly wisdom can cause a society to experience unprecedented prosperity and peace.

Outline:

> Verses 1-19 – Solomon established a simple but efficient system to govern his empire.
>
> Verses 20-28 – Israel experienced extraordinary prosperity and tranquility because of Solomon's wisdom.
>
> Verses 29-34 – Solomon recorded the insights and teachings that the Lord gave to him; he also instructed the leaders of the nations around him.

Prayer Focus: Lord, help me to never selfishly pursue Your wisdom, but to seize every opportunity to use it to bless others. Amen.

Notes:

Spiritual Journal:

Week: Twenty-two
Day: Wednesday
Book: I Kings
Chapter: Five
Memory Verse: Five
Principle: William Carey, the father of modern Protestant missions, is famous for his challenge, "Attempt big things for God; expect big things from God."
Outline:

Verses 1-18 – Solomon and Hiram, the king of Tyre, established an agreement in which materials from Lebanon were to be procured for the magnificent building project in Solomon's heart – a Temple unto the Most High God.

Prayer Focus: Lord, help me to tap into every resource You have made available for me in my quest to fulfill Your vision for my life. Amen.

Notes:

Spiritual Journal:

Week: Twenty-two
Day: Thursday
Book: I Kings
Chapter: Six
Memory Verse: Twelve
Principle: No matter how elaborate a temple we may be able to construct, the deciding factor concerning the abiding presence of the Lord is in our obedience to His ordinances.
Outline:
Verses 1-10 – The overwhelming superstructure of the Temple is described.
Verses 11-13 – God's commitment to inhabit the Temple had to do not with the impressiveness of the facility but with the righteous obedience of the worshippers.
Verses 14-38 – The magnificence of the internal structure and furnishings is described.
Prayer Focus: Lord, help me to always remember that You already live in heaven, so no gift I could offer is impressive to You and that You seek only my righteous obedience. Amen.
Notes:

Spiritual Journal:

Week: Twenty-two
Day: Friday
Book: I Kings
Chapter: Seven
Memory Verse: Fifty-one
Principle: The very nature of God is abundance to the point of extravagance; therefore, there should be no embarrassment in serving Him with exuberance.
Outline:
        Verses 1-12 – The public and personal buildings that Solomon constructed were undertaken in the grandest of style and dimension.
        Verses 13-14 – The best craftsman available was imported to fashion the designs for the projects.
        Verses 15-51 – The massive bronze pillars and the brass sea that stood before the Temple and the magnificent furnishings that were inside the Temple were constructed with careful attention to the smallest detail but no concern for the cost of the project.
Prayer Focus: Lord, help me to know how to properly balance my role as a good steward of Your resources yet at the same time take my human limitations off Your unlimited assets. Amen.
Notes:

Spiritual Journal:

Week: Twenty-three
Day: Monday
Book: I Kings
Chapter: Eight
Memory Verse: Twenty-three
Principle: Our God is merciful; if we confess our sins, He is faithful and just to forgive us our sins and cleanse us from all unrighteousness.
Outline:

Verses 1-13 – With great pomp, Solomon brought the Ark of the Covenant into the Temple. As he did, the anointing of the Lord descended into the Temple in such a powerful way that the priests were overwhelmed in His presence.

Verses 14-53 – In his prayer of dedication for the Temple, Solomon continued to make the point that God's dwelling place was in heaven. Even though he had just built the most beautiful building in the history of the human race, Solomon understood that God's majesty still superseded the best of human efforts. However, he also continued to affirm that God would indeed respond to man's repentant prayers. Isaiah 57:15 makes the point that God dwells in the lofty places of the universe <u>and</u> in the contrite hearts of His people.

Verses 54-61 – Solomon's admonition to the congregation was that they dedicate themselves to serve God loyally.

Verses 62-66 – The sacrifice and celebration at the dedication of the Temple lasted for two full weeks.

Prayer Focus: Lord, help me to always keep a contrite heart as Your true dwelling place. Amen.

Notes:

Spiritual Journal:

Week: Twenty-three
Day: Tuesday
Book: I Kings
Chapter: Nine
Memory Verse: Five
Principle: God has a good plan for those who will follow His directions; however, those who disobey are destined to calamity as a sign that they are in opposition to the will and commandments of God.
Outline:
Verses 1-9 – God appeared to Solomon and reaffirmed the covenant He had made with King David; however, He emphasized to Solomon that turning to other gods would negate the covenant and yield devastating results in which Israel and their magnificent Temple would become points of ridicule among the nations. Perhaps it was because He knew that Solomon would commit exactly this treasonous act that He gave him such a severe warning.

Verses 10-14 – Conflict arose between the kings of Israel and Tyre over the payment that Solomon gave to Hiram for all the supplies that he had provided for the building projects.

Verses 15-19 – The extensive building projects of King Solomon are listed.

Verses 20-24 – Solomon's work force came from among the Canaanites who inhabited his territory, but the Israelites were employed in the military and as civil servants of the government.

Verse 25 – Solomon made public sacrifice three times each year.

Verses 26-28 – Solomon's merchant fleet also became a source of great revenue for his kingdom.

Prayer Focus: Lord, help me to never trust in my accomplishments, but may my confidence always rest upon my obedience to You. Amen.
Notes:

Spiritual Journal:

Week: Twenty-three
Day: Wednesday
Book: I Kings
Chapter: Ten
Memory Verse: Twenty-three
Principle: God's plan for His people is that they would surpass their unbelieving peers in every measurable dimension of life.
Outline:

Verses 1-13 – The queen of Sheba was overwhelmed with Solomon's wisdom and the wealth of his kingdom.

Verses 14-22 – The excessive prosperity of Solomon's kingdom is depicted by the golden shields which adorned his house, the golden cups which he used at his table, the ivory and gold throne upon which he sat, and the treasures collected by his merchant marine.

Verses 23-24 – No other empire could compare to Solomon's kingdom as long he continued in the wisdom of the Lord.

Verses 25-29 – Solomon's wealth came from a number of sources of revenue including: taxes, gifts and tribute from neighboring kings, and commercial enterprises among the surrounding countries.

Prayer Focus: Lord, allow me to be an example to others of the blessings which come from serving You. I don't ask in selfishness that I might gain position or prosperity for myself, but in humility that I might be an example of Your goodness before others. Amen.

Notes:

Spiritual Journal:

Week: Twenty-three
Day: Thursday
Book: I Kings
Chapter: Eleven
Memory Verse: Thirty-four

Principle: Even though each individual and generation must pay for its own sins, a righteous person can establish a godly blessing that will, to some extent, cover his descendants even if they fall short in their own righteousness.

Outline:

>Verses 1-13 – Because Solomon allowed his foreign wives to influence him to serve their pagan gods, the Lord warned Solomon that the kingdom would be taken from him. However, He added that He would delay the demise of the kingdom in honor of the covenant which He had established with David.

>Verses 14-28 – Enemies began to rise up against Solomon, including Hadad (an Edomite who sought revenge for David's attack upon his people), Rezon (king of Syria), and Jeroboam (the captain over Solomon's labor forces).

>Verses 29-40 – The prophet of the Lord gave Jeroboam a sign that ten of the twelve tribes of Israel would be taken from Solomon and given to him as a judgment for Solomon's idolatry, but two tribes would be left with Solomon to honor David's loyalty. The Lord further spoke to Jeroboam that, if he would serve the Lord as David had, a covenant similar to the one given to David would be established with him.

>Verses 41-43 – Upon Solomon's death, his son Rehoboam ascended to the throne.

Prayer Focus: Lord, help me to establish a godly heritage for my descendants and not to corrupt the godly heritage left to me by my ancestors. Amen.

Notes:

Spiritual Journal:

Week: Twenty-three
Day: Friday
Book: I Kings
Chapter: Twelve
Memory Verse: Fifteen
Principle: Although God does not indiscriminately preordain our lives, He foreknows our future because He thoroughly understands our personality and knows the choices we will tend to make.
Outline:

Verses 1-11 – When Rehoboam came to Shechem (the political center of the northern portion of the kingdom) to establish his reign, the people asked him to lighten the taxes and other requirements placed on them by his father Solomon. Solomon's advisors agreed that it would be wise for him to grant their request; however, Rehoboam turned to his peers for counsel. These young men, the sons of the officials in Solomon's kingdom, had grown up in the lap of luxury as a result of the heavy taxation upon the common people; therefore, they did not understand the suffering of the general populace. Rather, they knew only the benefits they had enjoyed and were greedy for more for themselves and their children. Therefore, they advised Rehoboam to increase, rather than decrease, the tax burden.

Verses 12-16 – When Rehoboam announced his decision, the people of the northern portion of the kingdom rebelled against his reign.

Verses 17-24 – The tribes of Judah and Benjamin remained loyal to the new king – a logical choice because they were from the area which benefited most from Solomon's taxation policy in that all the tribute money flowed into their region and pockets. When the king raised forces from these two tribes to attack the rebellious tribes, the Lord sent a prophet to warn him not to attack. Surprisingly, the young king consented to the words of the prophet and called off the campaign.

Verses 25-33 – When Jeroboam became the leader in the northern region, he feared that his people would eventually return their loyalty to Rehoboam if they continued to travel to Jerusalem for the religious holidays and to offer their sacrifices to the Lord. Therefore, he instituted an alternate religion in his kingdom with altars conveniently located in the north and south of his territory so that the people would not continue to make the long pilgrimage to Jerusalem.

Prayer Focus: Lord, help me to know Your heart the way You know mine and to yield to Your plan for my life so that I don't have to suffer under the burden of Your indictment against my life. Amen.
Notes & Spiritual Journal:

Week: Twenty-four
Day: Monday
Book: I Kings
Chapter: Thirteen
Memory Verse: Twenty-six
Principle: Just because we may have spiritual gifts and supernatural manifestations does not mean that we are above sin and rebellion against the Lord.
Outline:

Verses 1-10 – A man of God from Judah came to Bethel to speak God's judgment against the idolatry in Israel. His remarkable prophecy even included the name of the king who would eventually burn the bones of the pagan priests on their own altar. When the king commanded that the man be arrested, his hand withered; however, as soon as he entreated the man of God, the hand was restored. The prophet refused the king's invitation to dinner, stating that he had specific instructions from the Lord to return home without stopping to eat.

Verses 11-22 – When a local prophet heard the news about the man's prophecy, he was able to convince the man of God to have a meal with him by saying that he had instructions from the Lord that the Judean prophet was to come share a meal with the local prophet. During this meal, the Word of the Lord came that the man of God had invited judgment upon himself through his disobedience.

Verses 23-32 – As the man of God traveled from Bethel, he was attacked and killed by a lion. As proof that this turn of events was supernatural, the lion did not devour the corpse nor did the donkey flee from the lion – in total contradiction to natural order. The prophet collected the corpse and had him buried in his own tomb with instructions that he would later be buried alongside this disobedient man of God.

Verses 33-34 – In spite of the supernatural warning and the miraculous sign of the affliction and restoration of his hand, Jeroboam did not repent of his idolatry that became a great sin among his people.

Prayer Focus: Lord, help me to have not only spiritual wisdom but also the common sense to turn from rebellion and wickedness. Amen.
Notes & Spiritual Journal:

Week: Twenty-four

Day: Tuesday

Book: I Kings

Chapter: Fourteen

Memory Verse: Sixteen

Principle: Our personal sins can cause a ripple effect which can bring disaster into the lives of those in our own family and those under our influence.

Outline:

Verses 1-18 – When Jeroboam's son became ill, the king sent his wife in disguise to inquire of the prophet concerning the child. The prophet not only discerned who it was that had come to him *incognito* but also foretold the child's death and the judgment which the Lord would bring upon Jeroboam's family because of his idolatry.

Verses 19-20 – After twenty-two years as king, Jeroboam died.

Verses 21-31 – Rehoboam's reign in Judah was also marked with wickedness and idolatry. When the Egyptians attacked the city of Jerusalem and took all the treasures of the Temple, Rehoboam replaced the gold shields with ones of bronze – symbolizing the degradation which had occurred under his rule. He died after serving as king for seventeen years.

Prayer Focus: Lord, lead me in the paths of righteousness and protect me from bringing myself and those I love under Your judgment. Amen.

Notes:

Spiritual Journal:

Week: Twenty-four
Day: Wednesday
Book: I Kings
Chapter: Fifteen
Memory Verse: Four
Principle: In this chapter, which begins to tell the history of the kings of Judah and Israel, we see both good and bad kings. One thing which is remarkably revealed is the long-lasting effects of sinfulness and righteousness: David's righteousness brought grace for Abijam even though he was unrighteous, and Jeroboam's wickedness brought judgment upon Nadab and his entire family because they also practiced wickedness.

Outline:

Verses 1-8 – Abijam ruled in Judah for three years. Even though his reign was marked with wickedness, God allowed him to remain because of the covenant He had made with King David.

Verses 9-24 – Asa's forty-one-year reign in Judah was a time of reform and spiritual renewal and purity. One of Asa's significant political moves was emptying the treasures of the government and the Temple in order to bribe the king of Syria into making war against the king of Israel, who was in the process of building a city to block the trade routes into Judah.

Verses 25-32 – Nadab came to power in Israel but was killed along with his entire family in a bloodbath at the hands of Baasha who then took the throne.

Verses 33-34 – During his twenty-four-year reign over Israel, Baasha led the nation in the idolatrous sins of Jeroboam.

Prayer Focus: Lord, lead me in the paths of righteousness, not only for my own sake, but also for the legacy that I can leave behind for others. Amen.

Notes:

Spiritual Journal:

Week: Twenty-four
Day: Thursday
Book: I Kings
Chapter: Sixteen
Memory Verse: Nineteen
Principle: No sin – unless it has been forgiven through Christ – will ever go unpunished. Numbers 32:23 declares that the sinner must be aware that his sins will find him out.
Outline:

>Verses 1-7 – God sent the prophet Jehu to declare to Baasha that, because of his sins, he would face a massacre similar to that had come upon Nadab.

>Verses 8-14 – Baasha's son Elah reigned in Israel for two years before he and his entire family were slaughtered by Zimri.

>Verses 15-20 – After seven days in power, Zimri was challenged by Omri, whose forces surrounded him in his citadel. Upon realizing that he was cornered, Zimri set the building afire and died in the blaze.

>Verses 21-28 – Although Omri's reign in Israel began with a challenge from Tibni, he soon established himself and ruled for twelve years. One significant move that he made during his time in power was the establishment of the city of Samaria. Unfortunately, he continued in the idolatrous sins of Jeroboam.

>Verses 29-34 – Omri's son Ahab succeeded him on the throne in the new capital of Samaria, where he ruled for twenty-two years. Not only did he continue the idolatrous traditions of his predecessors, he also married Jezebel, the daughter of the king of Sidon, and introduced the pagan religion from their nation to Israel.

Prayer Focus: Lord, when I am tempted with sin, help me to remember that consequences will come. Amen.
Notes:

Spiritual Journal:

Week: Twenty-four
Day: Friday
Book: I Kings
Chapter: Seventeen
Memory Verse: Two
Principle: Our lives can experience dramatic and unexpected changes when God speaks to us.
Outline:

Verses 1-7 – After he prophesied to King Ahab that there would be no rain or dew until he declared their return, the prophet Elijah took refuge at the Brook Cherith where he was supernaturally fed by ravens each day. However, the brook eventually dried up.

Verses 8-16 – Next, the prophet was led to Zarephath, a village in Sidon, where he met a widow who was collecting sticks to prepare the last bit of food she had left. When Elijah asked her to give him a cake, she retorted that she and her son were going to eat this last bit of food and then die of starvation. The prophet responded that, if she would obey his request, she would see a miracle – the little oil and meal she had would last throughout the rest of the famine. Her obedience was rewarded in what seems to be even a bigger miracle than was expected, in that the Scriptures record that her whole household – not just the son and herself – was fed from the supply.

Verses 17-24 – When the son became ill and died, the widow accused Elijah of bringing the distress upon her; however, the boy was restored to life through the prophet's prayers. The widow's response was surprising in that she declared that now she knew that the prophet's words were true. How could she have doubted after the miracle provision of the oil and meal?

Prayer Focus: Lord, help me to always listen for and respond to Your voice. Amen.
Notes:

Spiritual Journal:

Week: Twenty-five
Day: Monday
Book: I Kings
Chapter: Eighteen
Memory Verse: Twenty-one
Principle: We must make a definite decision in favor of Christ; making no decision is the same as deciding against Him.
Outline:

Verses 1-16 – Although Obadiah was a trusted servant of Ahab, he was devoted to the Lord and had hidden one hundred of the Lord's prophets when Jezebel had tried to kill them. When Obadiah was sent to look for water to sustain the king's horses, he encountered Elijah along the way. The prophet requested that he take a message to Ahab, but Obadiah feared that Elijah would disappear before the king was able to meet him, leaving Obadiah in danger of the king's wrath.

Verses 17-40 – When the king met with the prophet, Elijah proposed a challenge between himself and the prophets of Baal. The contest was held atop Mount Carmel where altars to God and Baal were erected, and sacrifices were made with the request that the true deity would send fire from heaven to consume the offering. The prophets of Baal spent all day entreating their god to send supernatural fire; however, nothing happened. When it came Elijah's turn, he made the challenge even more interesting by pouring twelve barrels of water over his sacrifice. Then, he asked God to send fire to consume the soggy offering. Supernatural fire instantly came and consumed not only the offering but also the altar, the water in the trenches around the altar, and the earth upon which the altar stood. At this great sign, Elijah had all the prophets and priests of Baal slain.

Verses 41-46 – Now that the false religion had been exposed, Elijah was ready to pray for rain to return to Israel. After seven requests, a cloud appeared, and Elijah knew that his prayers were being answered. He sent a message to the king that he needed to leave town; otherwise, he would be trapped in a flood.

Prayer Focus: Lord, help me to make the choice to recognize You as the only true and living God and to surrender myself to You as my only source of salvation and as my absolute Lord. Amen.
Notes & Spiritual Journal:

Week: Twenty-five
Day: Tuesday
Book: I Kings
Chapter: Nineteen
Memory Verse: Nine

Principle: Occasionally, we need to check ourselves and see where we are in life and what we are doing there. It is important that we constantly re-evaluate ourselves to see if we are on course with God's plan for our lives.

Outline:

Verses 1-8 – In fear, Elijah fled from Jezebel. He left his servant at Beersheba and journeyed further to a desert place where an angel appeared to him and gave him food to strengthen him for a forty-day trek to Mount Horeb.

Verses 9-14 – God appeared to the prophet at Mount Horeb – not in a spectacular wind, earthquake, or fire, but in a still, small voice.

Verses 15-18 – God gave the prophet new direction in life – to anoint new kings in Israel and Judah and a new prophet in the land.

Verses 19-21 – When Elijah threw his mantle across the shoulders of Elisha, he immediately recognized and surrendered to his prophetic calling.

Prayer Focus: Lord, help me to stop often enough for re-evaluation so that I can continually walk in Your direction for my life. Amen.

Notes:

Spiritual Journal:

Week: Twenty-five
Day: Wednesday
Book: I Kings
Chapter: Twenty
Memory Verse: Twenty-eight
Principle: God refuses to be "put into a box" and limited by our human reasoning. When
    we try to do so, we always find ourselves under His judgment and correction.
Outline:
    Verses 1-21 – Ben-hadad, king of Syria, decided to plunder Israel by demanding
        from King Ahab a ransom of all the gold and silver as well as his choicest
        wives and children. Once Ahab agreed to his demand, Ben-hadad
        increased the demands to include anything of worth in the homes of the
        king and his servants. At this turn of events, the elders of the country
        advised Ahab that he should not yield to the increased demands. When a
        prophet arose with a message from the Lord that the young leaders of the
        provinces could bring victory, Ahab decided to attack the king of Syria.
        The army of Israel enjoyed a great victory and Ben-hadad fled away.
    Verses 22-30 – Just as had been proclaimed by the prophet, Ben-hadad returned in
        the spring thinking that the first defeat had been because the battle had
        been joined in the hills and that God would not be able to give Israel the
        victory if the next encounter would be in the plains. However, a man of
        God prophesied that the Lord would prove Himself victorious regardless
        of the terrain in which the battle was staged. Indeed, the enemy was
        routed and the king was blockaded in an inner chamber in Aphek.
    Verses 31-34 – When some of Ben-hadad's servants went to King Ahab to beg
        that the life of Ben-hadad be spared, the king of Israel answered favorably
        and a meeting between the two kings was arranged. The Syrian king made
        certain concessions to the Israelite king, and he was released to return to
        his home.
    Verses 35-43 – One of the company of the prophets disguised himself and
        arranged to be in the path of King Ahab's chariot. When the king stopped,
        the prophet told a story of how he was to be executed because he had
        allowed a prisoner of war to escape. When the king concurred with the
        judgment, the prophet revealed himself and pronounced judgment upon
        Ahab for allowing Ben-hadad to escape.
Prayer Focus: Lord, help me to "think outside the box" and tap into Your unlimited
    wisdom. Amen.
Notes & Spiritual Journal:

Week: Twenty-five
Day: Thursday
Book: I Kings
Chapter: Twenty-one
Memory Verse: Twenty
Principle: There is no hidden sin which will not be exposed.
Outline:

        Verses 1-16 – Ahab desired to purchase the vineyard of Naboth because it was next to the royal palace. Naboth refused to sell the property because it was his inheritance that he desired to protect according to the commandment given in Numbers 36:7. When Jezebel saw how discouraged Ahab was over not being able to obtain the property, she arranged to have false accusations brought against Naboth so that he would be executed and the property relinquished to the king.

        Verses 17-26 – When Ahab went to the vineyard to claim it for himself, the prophet Elijah met him there and spoke severe judgment upon him, Jezebel, and their entire family.

        Verses 27-29 – Because Ahab expressed sincere remorse, God allowed a temporary stay on the judgment so that it came during the reign of his son.

Prayer Focus: Lord, help me to live totally open before You without the self-deception that I can hide anything from You and escape the deserved judgment. Amen.

Notes:

Spiritual Journal:

Week: Twenty-five
Day: Friday
Book: I Kings
Chapter: Twenty-two
Memory Verse: Seven
Principle: In every decision in life – whether great or small – we should seek God's wisdom and the counsel of God's spokesmen.
Outline:
> Verses 1-28 – When Jehoshaphat, king of Judah, visited Ahab, king of Israel, Ahab asked him to join with him in a campaign against Syria to take possession of the city of Ramoth Gilead. Jehoshaphat eagerly agreed but asked if there was a prophet of the Lord from whom to inquire advice before launching the attack. Ahab brought out four hundred prophets who would speak favorably of his plans, but Jehoshaphat asked if there might be one more prophet to consult. Although Ahab was unwilling to call Micaiah because he always contradicted the king's plans, he summoned him by a messenger, who advised the prophet to speak favorably as did all the rest of the prophets. Micaiah mockingly spoke soothing words at first but shifted to the truth when the king admonished him. The king refused Micaiah's verdict and had the prophet imprisoned. One section of this story which often seems to perplex Bible students is the story of the lying spirit which the Lord permitted to enter the mouths of the prophets. Many question how a holy God could send a lying spirit to do His work. However, if this passage is considered in light of the book of Job, where we learn that Satan appeared before God and asked permission to harass Job, we get a new comprehension of authority in the spiritual realm. Apparently, the demonic forces are not free to operate at will in the earth; they must – in some cases, at least – obtain permission from God before they make their forays in the world.
> Verses 29-40 – Ignoring the word of the prophet, the kings of Judah and Israel launched an attack upon the king of Syria. Ahab went into battle dressed as an enlisted soldier while Jehoshaphat wore his regal attire. At first, the enemy focused on Jehoshaphat, thinking him to be the king of Israel. When it was discovered that he was not Ahab, one soldier shot an arrow at random which fatally wounded the king of Israel. After the king's body was removed from the chariot, dogs licked his blood from the floor of the chariot in fulfillment of the words of the prophet.
> Verses 41-50 – Jehoshaphat succeeded his father on the throne in Judah and ruled for twenty-five years with a reign which was marked with righteousness.
> Verses 51-53 – Ahaziah succeeded his father Ahab on the throne of Israel and ruled for two years with a reign which was marked by wickedness and idolatry.
Prayer Focus: Lord, help me always to hear Your counsel concerning the decisions which I must make – but most of all, help me to follow the counsel You give me. Amen.
Notes & Spiritual Journal:

Week: Twenty-six
Day: Monday
Book: II Kings
Chapter: One
Memory Verse: Sixteen
Principle: God has the ultimate word on every topic, and there is no need to seek counsel
    elsewhere.
Outline:

    Verses 1-8 – When King Ahaziah was injured in a fall, he sent messengers to
    Baalzebub to inquire concerning the outcome of his condition. Elijah met
    the messengers along the way and commanded them to return to the king
    with the question as to why he did not inquire of the Lord rather than a
    pagan deity and with the verdict that the king would not recover from his
    injury. Ahaziah was angry when he was able to determine that the
    message had come from the prophet Elijah.

    Verses 9-14 – The king sent an officer with fifty soldiers to bring Elijah into
    custody; however, the prophet called down fire from heaven to consume
    them. The same scenario was repeated with the second band of men
    charged to bring in the prophet. When a third band was commissioned
    with the job, the officer humbly begged for Elijah's mercy.

    Verses 15-16 – After an angel appeared to the prophet and reassured him that he
    could safely appear before the king, Elijah personally delivered the verdict
    to Ahaziah.

    Verses 17-18 – The king died exactly as the prophet had foretold.
Prayer Focus: Lord, help me to rely upon You and You alone. Amen.
Notes:

Spiritual Journal:

Week: Twenty-six
Day: Tuesday
Book: II Kings
Chapter: Two
Memory Verse: Fourteen
Principle: Too often, we relegate the great acts of God to history and fail to believe that we can have God's power and authority manifest in our lives with the same intensity as that which biblical characters and the great men of faith in history experienced.

Outline:

Verses 1-6 – Even though Elijah requested that his disciple tarry at various places along the way, Elisha was determined to stay with his master until the very last minute possible.

Verses 7-10 – Elijah parted the waters of the Jordan by striking them with his mantle. When Elisha asked for a double portion of the anointing that was manifest in Elijah's life and ministry, the prophet directed that he would receive his request if he saw him when he ascended to heaven.

Verses 11-14 – When Elijah was taken up in a whirlwind accompanied by the fiery chariot and horses, Elisha took the prophet's mantle and immediately put it to use by parting the waters of the Jordan just as he had seen his master do.

Verses 15-18 – When the sons of the prophets begged for permission to search for Elijah's body, Elisha yielded to their demands but was convinced that he would not be found because he knew that the prophet had gone into heaven.

Verses 19-22 – Upon his arrival at Jericho, Elisha found that the water supply of the city was tainted, and he miraculously cured it.

Verses 23-25 – As he traveled toward Carmel where he was to live, Elisha met a gang of forty-two mocking young men; as punishment for their disrespect for God's anointing and God's chosen minister, wild bears came from the woods and attacked the young men.

Prayer Focus: Lord, never let me be content to consider Your miraculous power as a fact of history; rather, help me to have faith to draw it into the present and see it manifest in my own life and ministry. Amen.

Notes & Spiritual Journal:

Week: Twenty-six
Day: Wednesday
Book: II Kings
Chapter: Three
Memory Verse: Eighteen
Principle: What seems impossible for men is simple for God.
Outline:

        Verses 1-5 – When Jehoram succeeded his father on the throne of Israel, the king of Moab refused to continue paying the tribute of lambs and wool which he had rendered regularly to Ahab.

        Verses 6-10 – The kings of Judah and of Edom joined Jehoram in his attack upon the Moabites; however, their assault seemed doomed from the first because there was no water to sustain the army or their cattle as they marched toward the battlefield.

        Verses 11-14 – Upon Jehoshaphat's request, the three kings were granted an audience with Elisha, who taunted Jehoram by questioning why he didn't inquire of the prophets who had served Ahab and Jezebel. The prophet made it plain that it was only his respect for the king of Judah that moved him to meet with Jehoram.

        Verses 15-19 – After a musician was called to play before the prophet, Elisha received the direction from the Lord that the armies should dig trenches which God would miraculously fill with water for the men and their animals. He further predicted victory for the armies and gave them instructions to totally devastate the land of Moab.

        Verses 20-25 – When the Moabites saw the morning sun reflected in the water that God had supernaturally supplied, they thought it to be blood and assumed that the three armies had fought against one another and annihilated themselves. They then went, apparently unarmed, onto the battlefield to take the spoil that they thought would be scattered among the corpses of the fallen soldiers. This turn of events allowed the three armies to ambush the Moabites and to follow through with the advice of the prophet concerning devastating the land.

        Verses 26-27 – When the king of Moab sacrificed his own son, the armies retreated.

Prayer Focus: Lord, help me to always face every problem with my confidence in Your ability, not my own. Amen.

Notes & Spiritual Journal:

Week: Twenty-six
Day: Thursday
Book: II Kings
Chapter: Four
Memory Verse: Twenty-six
Principle: Positive faith does not deny the facts but looks beyond the facts to the reality that God is in control and that He has a plan for a good end product for every calamity we face.
Outline:
Verses 1-7 – When the widow of one of the prophets faced bankruptcy and the conscription of her sons into slavery, the prophet predicted a miraculous multiplication of oil which she was able to sell to cover her debts.
Verses 8-37 – When a wealthy woman of Shunem befriended the prophet, he predicted that she would bear a son. When this boy was several years old, he fell ill with an apparent heatstroke and died. When the mother rushed to the prophet for help, she continued to demonstrate great faith with her proclamation that all was well as she honestly faced the present fact that the boy was dead. Through Elijah's prayers, the boy was miraculously raised to life again.
Verses 38-41 – Elijah threw meal into a pot of stew containing poison vegetables and made it harmless for the sons of the prophets to eat.
Verses 42-44 – Through obedience to the word of the prophet, a man of Baal-Shalisha fed one hundred men with just twenty small barley cakes.
Prayer Focus: Lord, help me to know the difference between faith, foolishness, and presumption so that I can always walk in positive faith no matter what the present circumstances may be. Amen.
Notes:

Spiritual Journal:

Week: Twenty-six
Day: Friday
Book: II Kings
Chapter: Five
Memory Verse: Eight
Principle: God wants to work through His people miraculously as proof that He really is God and that His people really are different from the rest of the world.

Outline:

Verses 1-7 – When the king of Syria sent one of his top officers to Israel to be healed of leprosy, the king of Israel thought that it was an attempt to trick him.

Verses 8-12 – The prophet sent word to the king that he was willing to heal the Syrian and instructed Naaman to dip in the Jordan River seven times in order to be cleansed.

Verses 13-19 – At first, Naaman refused the prophet's advice, but he later consented to the prodding of his servants and was healed when he washed in the river. In appreciation, he offered a reward to the prophet. When Elisha refused the payment, Naaman made one simple request, that he be granted earth from Israel to take back to Syria so that he could kneel on Israelite soil even when he had to accompany the king of Syria into the pagan Temple.

Verses 20-27 – Moved with greed, Elisha's servant deceived Naaman into giving him gifts. When Gehazi returned, the prophet confronted him for his sin and called the leprosy which had gone from Naaman to come upon the wicked servant.

Prayer Focus: Lord, may I always be a vessel through whom You can prove Yourself to this generation. Amen.

Notes:

Spiritual Journal:

Week: Twenty-seven

Day: Monday

Book: II Kings

Chapter: Six

Memory Verse: Sixteen

Principle: Because we see only the physical evidence, we may not know all that God is doing behind the scenes on our behalf; however, we can certainly rest assured that He has more going for us than our enemy has going against us.

Outline:

Verses 1-7 – While Elisha's students were felling trees for lumber for their new facility, one lost a borrowed axe head in the river. At the prophet's command, the iron instrument floated to the surface to be retrieved.

Verses 8-12 – Through the word of knowledge, the prophet was able to know the Syrian king's attack plans and warn the king of Israel in advance of the planned attacks. When Ben-hadad questioned his counselors as to who was leaking security information to the Israelites, they advised him that the prophet was supernaturally discerning the secrets.

Verses 13-23 – In an unusual twist of events, the sightless were caused to see and the seeing were made sightless. When the great army that the Syrian king sent to capture Elisha surrounded him and his servant at Dothan, the servant was fearful. At the prophet's request, the Lord opened the servant's eyes to see the hosts of heaven who were arrayed on their side; also at the prophet's request, the eyes of the Syrians were blinded so that they were able to be led away captive to Samaria where they were brought to the king of Israel. Elisha convinced the king not to kill them but to feed them and release them as an act of courtesy to the prisoners of war.

Verses 24-30 – During a subsequent invasion by the Syrians, the city of Samaria was blockaded to the point that the people were starving and even turned to cannibalism to exist.

Verses 31-33 – The king of Israel blamed the prophet for the calamity and sent messengers to capture him.

Prayer Focus: Lord, help me to possess the spirit of wisdom and revelation and to have my spiritual eyes opened so that I can see what You are doing in and for me. (Ephesians 1:17-19) Amen.

Notes & Spiritual Journal:

Week: Twenty-seven
Day: Tuesday
Book: II Kings
Chapter: Seven
Memory Verse: Two
Principle: We must live in faith toward God, or else He will perform His mighty acts before us and we will not be allowed to benefit from them.
Outline:

Verses 1-2 – When Elisha prophesied to the king's assistant that God would end the famine and provide abundantly within one day's time, the officer refused to believe that it was possible. The prophet's response was that he would see the miracle but not be allowed to benefit from it.

Verses 3-11 – When four starving lepers decided to go to the Syrian camp to beg for their mercy, they were surprised to find the camp abandoned. God had caused the army to hear the sound of approaching horses and chariots, and they had fled for their lives. After their initial reaction of taking provisions for themselves, the lepers realized that they must get the news to the king of Israel.

Verses 12-16 – After a preliminary response of concern that the Syrians had set a trap for the people of Israel, the king decided to send men to investigate the report of the lepers.

Verses 17-20 – The king appointed the officer who had first visited Elisha to collect payment from the people as they went into the Syrian camp to take the provisions; however, the people rushed the gate so forcefully that the officer was trampled under their onslaught – fulfilling the word of the prophet that he would see the Lord's miraculous provision but not be able to take advantage of it.

Prayer Focus: Lord, help me to always be in faith so that I not only see Your hand at work but also receive from that gracious hand. Amen.
Notes:

Spiritual Journal:

Week: Twenty-seven
Day: Wednesday
Book: II Kings
Chapter: Eight
Memory Verse: Four
Principle: As we read the stories in the books entitled "Kings," we can see that the real driving force of history was not actually the kings but the prophets. It is the man on his knees, not the man on the throne, who shapes destiny.
Outline:

Verses 1-6 – The Shunammite woman's land was confiscated when she lived abroad for seven years during a famine. When she returned and went to the king to petition that it be returned to her, Gehazi was in the king's chamber reciting the stories of Elisha's great deeds. Because the king had just heard of the raising of her son from death, he was favorable to her and demanded that all her property be restored to her. This is an interesting turn of events since Elisha had once asked the lady if she would desire him to speak to the king on her behalf.

Verses 7-15 – When Ben-hadad fell sick, he sent Hazael to inquire of Elisha concerning his recovery. The prophet's response was that Hazael would give the king a favorable report – a truth in that the king was not to die of the disease which had brought him to his bed.However, Hazael's intent was to assassinate the king and rule in his place. The prophet not only foresaw the assassination, he also predicted the destruction that the new king would bring against the people of Israel.

Verses 16-24 – Jehoram succeeded his father Jehoshaphat and reigned for eight years. He married Athaliah, the daughter of Ahab and Jezebel, and led Judah into the sins of Israel to the extent that God desired to destroy the nation; however, He spared them because of the covenant He had made with King David.

Verses 25-29 – At Jehoram's death, his son Ahaziah took the throne. His reign was marked with a close association to Israel because Athaliah, his mother, was from the royal family of the northern kingdom and because he also married into that family. In an action reminiscent of his grandfather Jehoshaphat, He joined with Joram, king of Israel, in battle against Syria at Ramoth Gilead.

Prayer Focus: Lord, help me to never set my attention on the temporal powers which seem to dominate the present situation. Help me to rather keep my focus on the spiritual principles that rule not only the present but also the future. Amen.
Notes & Spiritual Journal:

Week: Twenty-seven
Day: Thursday
Book: II Kings
Chapter: Nine
Memory Verse: Twenty-six
Principle: God has a way of repaying our deeds and usually with an ironic twist so that it is unmistakable that it is the hand of the Lord at work – not just a coincidence. He said that the one who digs a pit will be the one who will fall into it.
Outline:

Verses 1-9 – Elisha sent one of the sons of the prophets to Jehu, the son of Jehoshaphat, to anoint him as the next king over Israel. When the young prophet met the future king, he foretold how that he would be responsible for the total destruction of the present evil ruling house.

Verses 10-13 – When Jehu disclosed the prophecy to the captains of the army, they immediately proclaimed their support for him and sprang into action to put him into power.

Verses 14-29 – Jehu rushed to Ramoth Gilead to attack Joram. When it became apparent that his aim was to displace the king, even the envoys whom Joram sent to him joined with Jehu. When the king of Israel and the king of Judah came out to face Jehu, Jehu killed Joram and threw his body into the field that his father had stolen from Naboth. Next, he killed Ahaziah, whose body was taken back to Jerusalem for burial.

Verses 30-37 – Entering the city of Jezreel, Jehu called for someone inside the palace to join his side and throw Jezebel from her window. The eunuchs in her chamber responded and hurled the queen to her death. Her body was trampled by the horses and ravaged by the dogs to the point that there were not enough pieces left intact for burial.

Prayer Focus: Lord, help me to live my life so that You can always leave Your distinctive mark of blessing rather than Your telltale mark of judgment on me. Amen.

Notes:

Spiritual Journal:

Week: Twenty-seven

Day: Friday

Book: II Kings

Chapter: Ten

Memory Verse: Thirty-one

Principle: Although God will commend us and reward us for our obedience, He cannot give us the fullness of His kingdom unless we diligently follow after Him in every area of obedience.

Outline:

Verses 1-11 – Jehu challenged the supporters of Ahab's family to try to establish one of his seventy sons on the throne. When they responded that they would not stand against Jehu, he responded that they had to kill all seventy heirs and send their heads to him as proof of their loyalty.

Verses 12-14 – Jehu then executed all forty-two of Ahaziah's brothers.

Verses 15-17 – In fulfillment of the prophecy of Elijah, Jehu destroyed all the remnant of Ahab's household.

Verses 18-28 – By calling a great sacrifice to Baal, Jehu was able to gather all the idolatrous devotees together for a great slaughter.

Verses 29-36 – In spite of Jehu's zeal in destroying Baal worship in Israel, he fell short of following the Lord wholeheartedly in that he did not stop the calf worship that Jeroboam had instituted in Bethel and Dan. Though God blessed Jehu's house for four generations because of his zeal against Baal, the enemies of the nation were able to begin to take territory away from the land because God's full blessing was held back.

Prayer Focus: Lord, I know that You gave Your all for me; help me to always give You one hundred percent of my life, loyalty, and dedication. Amen.

Notes:

Spiritual Journal:

Week: Twenty-eight
Day: Monday
Book: II Kings
Chapter: Eleven
Memory Verse: Seventeen
Principle: The political leaders of a people strongly influence – and can even determine – the religious convictions of their followers.
Outline:

> Verses 1-3 – At Ahaziah's death, Athaliah took power and massacred all the possible heirs who might challenge her for the throne. However, the infant Joash was hidden from her.
>
> Verses 4-12 – When Joash turned seven years old, Jehoiada the priest staged a coup against Athaliah and presented the lad to the people as their king.
>
> Verses 13-16 – The Temple guards executed Athaliah.
>
> Verses 17-21 – The first act of the new seven-year-old king was to enter into covenant with the people and with God, declaring that the Lord would be the God of the people. The nation responded immediately by destroying the Temple of Baal and killing the priests who served there.

Prayer Focus: Lord, whether as a leader or as a follower, help me always to remember that it is necessary to establish the Lord as the head of the nation as well as the head of my own life. Amen.

Notes:

Spiritual Journal:

Week: Twenty-eight
Day: Tuesday
Book: II Kings
Chapter: Twelve
Memory Verse: Two
Principle: Success in life depends upon following the Lord's directions, but sometimes we need a mentor to help do that.
Outline:

Verses 1-16 – Probably, Jehoash's greatest accomplishment was the repair of the Temple. When the original plan for funding his repair program failed, the king set up a box in the Temple to collect money that went directly into the hands of the construction crew. These funds covered all the structural repairs but did not fund the replacement of utensils used in worship.

Verses 17-18 – Jehoash took all the gold and treasures from the Temple in order to make a tribute payment to the king of Syria to turn him away from attacking Jerusalem.

Verses 19-21 – Apparently in connection with his plunder of the Temple treasury, Jehoash's servants assassinated him and placed his son on the throne.

Prayer Focus: Lord, help me to do righteously not just when I am under the direction of a human mentor but also because I am constantly led by Your Holy Spirit. Amen.
Notes:

Spiritual Journal:

Week: Twenty-eight
Day: Wednesday
Book: II Kings
Chapter: Thirteen
Memory Verse: Twenty-three
Principle: The graciousness and compassion of the Lord exceed His righteous judgment. He often extends the grace that He appropriates to the righteous for generations even though the heirs may be unrighteous.
Outline:

Verses 1-9 – Jehoahaz ruled Israel after the death of his father Jehu. During his reign, which was marked with wickedness and idolatry, the Syrians severely oppressed the people of Israel. Because the king besought the Lord, He sent a savior who delivered the nation even though the military force was almost depleted.

Verses 10-13 – Joash succeeded his father Jehoahaz as king of Israel. His reign was also wicked.

Verses 14-19 – As Elisha neared death, King Joash came to visit him. During the visit, the prophet gave him a sign concerning his conquests of the enemy. Because the king only struck the ground three times, he was allowed to recapture only three cities from the enemy.

Verses 20-21 – Almost a year after Elisha's death, the body of a soldier was tossed into his sepulcher. When the corpse touched the prophet's bones, the soldier came back to life. It is interesting to note that this last miracle – performed after the prophet's death – brought the listing of recorded miracles in his life to exactly double those recorded in the life of Elijah. This was likely a fulfillment of his request for a double portion of his mentor's anointing.

Verses 22-25 – Although the present generation really did not deserve the Lord's favor, He granted them mercy because of their righteous heritage.

Prayer Focus: Lord, help me not to be one who has to rely upon my father's blessings, but to be one who establishes a heritage for future generations to draw from. Amen.

Notes:

Spiritual Journal:

Week: Twenty-eight
Day: Thursday
Book: II Kings
Chapter: Fourteen
Memory Verse: Twenty-seven
Principle: God always has a good plan for His people. If necessary, He will even use evil
people to fulfill it.
Outline:
Verses 1-14 – When Amaziah ascended the throne in Judah, he avenged the assassination of his father by executing all those who plotted against him to take his life. He then went to battle against Edom and succeeded; however, this conquest caused him to become over-confident to the point that he challenged the king of Israel to battle. His defeat at the hand of Jehoash led to the breaching of the walls of Jerusalem and the plunder of the treasures of both the Temple and the king's house.

Verses 15-22 – Amaziah outlived Jehoash by fifteen years but was killed by conspirators from his own city. His son Azariah replaced him in power.

Verses 23-29 – Jeroboam succeeded his father Jehoash in Israel. Even though he was an evil king who led the people into idolatry, God used him to bring increase to the nation in fulfillment of the words of the prophet and the desire of His own heart that His people not be afflicted.

Prayer Focus: Lord, thank You for the undeserved mercies and blessings You channel into my life, even through the most unexpected avenues. Amen.
Notes:

Spiritual Journal:

Week: Twenty-eight
Day: Friday
Book: II Kings
Chapter: Fifteen
Memory Verse: Four
Principle: The Lord is looking for whole-hearted obedience.
Outline:

> Verses 1-7 – Azariah (Uzziah) ruled Judah righteously for fifty-two years, yet failed to follow the Lord perfectly.
>
> Verses 8-12 – Zachariah ruled Israel only six months before he was assassinated.
>
> Verses 13-15 – Shallum, who had murdered Zachariah, reigned for only one month before he was also assassinated.
>
> Verses 16-22 – Menahem's ten-year reign in Israel was most significantly marked by the tribute which was extracted by Assyria resulting in his having to levy taxes on all the citizens.
>
> Verses 23-26 – Pekahiah ruled Israel for two years until he was killed by Pekah, in order to take the throne from him.
>
> Verses 27-31 – Pekah's twenty-year reign was highlighted by the invasion by Tiglath-Pileser, who took the people of Israel captive and made them slaves in Assyria. Pekah lost his throne and life in a conspiracy led by Hoshea.
>
> Verses 32-38 – Jotham succeeded his father Uzziah (Azariah) on the throne in Judah. Like his father, he ruled righteously but allowed the high places to remain. During his reign, the Syrians and Israelites began to arm themselves against the nation of Judah.

Prayer Focus: Lord, help me to never stop halfway – or even ninety-nine percent of the way – when following You. Amen.
Notes:

Spiritual Journal:

Week: Twenty-nine

Day: Monday

Book: II Kings

Chapter: Sixteen

Memory Verse: Seven

Principle: Jesus called us to be in the world but not to be part of it. When we identify with the unregenerate, we lose our identity with and in Christ.

Outline:

> Verses 1-4 – Ahaz became the next king of Judah; however, he led the nation into the sins of idolatry, which were common in Israel – even including child sacrifice.
>
> Verses 5-9 – To defend his nation against the attacks of Israel and Syria, Ahaz aligned himself with Assyria and paid heavy tribute to them.
>
> Verses 10-16 – Ahaz had an altar built after the pattern of the pagan altar that was in Damascus. As soon as the altar was in place, the sacrifice system was altered to include offerings on it.
>
> Verses 17-18 – He also removed the oxen from the laver and the Sabbath court as part of the tribute to the Assyrians.
>
> Verses 19-20 – Ahaz died after sixteen years in power.

Prayer Focus: Lord, I pray for myself the same prayer that Jesus prayed for the whole Body of Christ, *I pray not that You should take them out of the world, but that You should keep them from the evil.* Amen.

Notes:

Spiritual Journal:

Week: Twenty-nine
Day: Tuesday
Book: II Kings
Chapter: Seventeen
Memory Verse: Thirty-five
Principle: The *shema*, Israel's principal statement of doctrine states, *Hear, O Israel: The LORD our God is one LORD.* The following verse completes the thought by adding, *And you shall love the LORD thy God with all your heart, and with all your soul, and with all your might.*
Outline:
> Verses 1-2 – Hoshea became the next king of Israel and led the people in wickedness, though not as severely as some of his predecessors.
>
> Verses 3-6 – The Assyrians attacked and captured Israel because they had aligned themselves with Egypt and had refused to pay their annual tribute.
>
> Verses 7-23 – The direct cause of Israel's calamity was their idolatry and their disobedience to the Lord's ordinances.
>
> Verses 24-41 – The expatriates who were brought in to inhabit the land of Israel brought with them their own religions and began to build altars to their foreign gods. When wild beasts began to attack, they decided that they needed to establish worship to the true God; however, this was done only half-heartedly, and the pagan worship continued in violation of the covenant of God.

Prayer Focus: Lord, help me to live not only by the Old Testament mandate to serve only the one true God but to remember that the same definition of the faith is given in the New Testament as well, *One Lord, one faith, one baptism, one God and Father of all, who is above all, and through all, and in you all.* (Ephesians 4:5) Amen.
Notes:

Spiritual Journal:

Week: Twenty-nine

Day: Wednesday

Book: II Kings

Chapter: Eighteen

Memory Verse: Five

Principle: In the book of Revelation, Satan is called "the accuser of the brethren." In this chapter, we see an excellent example of how we can be challenged in our faith and how we may have to withstand untrue accusations once we decide to trust in the Lord.

Outline:

> Verses 1-12 – When Hezekiah became king over Judah, he trusted wholly in the Lord, and God caused him to prosper even when the nations around him were suffering devastation at the hands of the Assyrians.

> Verses 13-16 – When Sennacherib turned toward Jerusalem, Hezekiah tried to peaceably defuse the situation by paying heavy tribute to the Assyrian king, emptying the government and Temple treasuries and even stripping the gold from the Temple doors.

> Verses 17-37 – The Assyrian messenger stood before the walls of Jerusalem and hurled accusations against Hezekiah, deliberately using the Hebrew so as to strike fear into the hearts of all the guards on the wall. They challenged the people of Israel not to believe that the Egyptians could deliver them and especially threatened them that trusting in the Lord was useless. They offered the military captains horses if they thought that they could mount an army to challenge the Assyrian forces. Then they offered the people a new country if they would surrender and go peacefully with their captors.

Prayer Focus: Lord, help me to always be able to discern and resist the accusations, threats, and lying promises of the enemy. Amen.

Notes:

Spiritual Journal:

Week: Twenty-nine
Day: Thursday
Book: II Kings
Chapter: Nineteen
Memory Verse: Six

Principle: We have already learned that our enemy is called *the accuser of the brethren.* The Bible also calls him *a liar* and *the father of lies.* Knowing this, our only legitimate response to him is to refuse to believe his lies and to trust instead the truthfulness of God.

Outline:

Verses 1-7 – In desperation, Hezekiah sent a messenger to ask Isaiah to inquire of the Lord concerning the Assyrian threat. The prophet's response was that God would cause the enemy king to hear a rumor that would cause him to retreat.

Verses 8-19 – When the Assyian king retreated, he sent a threatening letter to Hezekiah warning him that, just because he had pulled back, did not guarantee safety; he intended to come back and take the city – and even God would not stop him! Hezekiah responded by taking the letter into the Temple, spreading it before the Lord, and seeking His opinion on the matter.

Verses 20-31 – Isaiah sent a prophetic message to Hezekiah explaining that the pride of Israel was the reason that He had allowed the devastation of the Assyrian attack. He, however, reassured the nation that God had not forgotten them and that a remnant would be preserved and restored. As a sign that the prophecy was true, the prophet declared that the people would have to eat that year and the next of what they could forage but would be able to plant and reap a harvest in the third year.

Verses 32-34 – The prophecy continued that the Assyrians would not be able to enter the city because the Lord would protect Jerusalem for His own sake and for the sake of His servant David.

Verses 35-37 – When the Lord sent a plague that killed 185,000 of his army in one night, Sennacherib retreated to the Assyrian capital of Nineveh, where he was assassinated by his own sons.

Prayer Focus: Lord, help me to live by Your Word, which guarantees that even if all men are liars, You are true. Amen.

Notes & Spiritual Journal:

Week: Twenty-nine
Day: Friday
Book: II Kings
Chapter: Twenty
Memory Verse: Two
Principle: The only place to turn when "all hell breaks loose" is toward heaven.
Outline:

>> Verses 1-7 – When Hezekiah was seriously ill, Isaiah came to him with the Word of the Lord that he would die from the sickness. However, once the king prayed and wept before the Lord, God sent the prophet back with the message that God had heard his prayers and, for the sake of King David and for His own sake, He would extend the king's life for fifteen years.

>> Verses 8-11 – When Hezekiah requested a sign that the second word was truly from the Lord, the prophet asked God to miraculously turn the time backwards on the sundial.

>> Verses 12-19 – When the king of Babylon sent emissaries to congratulate Hezekiah on his miraculous recovery, he welcomed them with open arms and showed them all the wealth of his kingdom. Isaiah reprimanded the king for this openness, warning him that the Babylonians would someday return to plunder the kingdom of all the treasures they had seen.

>> Verses 20-21 – At the death of Hezekiah, his son Manasseh ascended to the throne of Judah. It is interesting to note that Manasseh, who was born during the fifteen years that were added to Hezekiah's life, was a very evil king. Perhaps Hezekiah would have been better off to have accepted the early death, avoiding the incident with the Babylonian spies and the birth of this wicked son.

Prayer Focus: Lord, give me faith to call upon You for help when I need it and wisdom to know the difference between the times when I really need You to change things and when all I really need is to trust Your plan. Amen.

Notes:

Spiritual Journal:

Week: Thirty
Day: Monday
Book: II Kings
Chapter: Twenty-one
Memory Verse: Twelve
Principle: Blatant sin and rebellion will certainly invoke God's most severe judgment.
Outline:

> Verses 1-9 – Manasseh's fifty-five-year reign was marked with blatant sin and patent idolatry.
>
> Verses 10-15 – The Lord sent prophetic messengers who warned of the severe impending judgment that would astonish all who even heard of it.
>
> Verse 16 – Manasseh added the murder of the innocent, likely including the prophets who came to warn him, to his list of atrocities.
>
> Verses 17-18 – At Manasseh's death, his son Amon ascended to the throne.
>
> Verses 19-26 – Amon followed the evil ways of his father; however, his reign was terminated by his assassination after just two years.

Prayer Focus: Lord, thank You for Your mercy which You constantly extend toward me, but I also ask that You help me to never fool myself into thinking that I can sin and yet avoid Your judgment. Amen.

Notes:

Spiritual Journal:

Week: Thirty
Day: Tuesday
Book: II Kings
Chapter: Twenty-two
Memory Verse: Nineteen
Principle: It is possible to escape the judgment that God levies upon the wicked by humbling ourselves before Him and seeking His forgiveness.
Outline:

Verses 1-2 – Josiah had a righteous relationship with the Lord and followed Him with his whole heart.

Verses 3-8 – When Josiah sent his scribe to Hilkiah to oversee the payment of the workmen repairing the Temple, the priest gave him a copy of the Book of the Law (likely Deuteronomy) which had been uncovered during the Temple renovations.

Verses 9-11 – When the king heard the words of the Law and realized how seriously his people had violated the Lord's commands, he ripped his clothes as a sign of his anguish.

Verses 12-20 – The king sent an envoy back to the priest to inquire of the Lord concerning the impending judgment. The Lord's response was that the people would, indeed, be judged harshly because of their sinful rebellion; however, because of the king's repentant heart, he would die peaceably before this calamity would come upon the nation.

Prayer Focus: Lord, help me to have the testimony of Josiah that I did not turn to the right or left from serving You and that my heart was always tender before You. Amen.
Notes:

Spiritual Journal:

Week: Thirty
Day: Wednesday
Book: II Kings
Chapter: Twenty-three
Memory Verse: Three
Principle: Proverbs 14:34 proclaims, *Righteousness exalteth a nation: but sin is a reproach to any people.* It is God's desire that the leadership of every community set a standard of righteousness for the citizenry to follow.
Outline:

> Verses 1-3 – Josiah called a mass assembly together to hear the reading of the Book of the Covenant. He then made a public demonstration of his covenant with the Lord to fulfill the commandments of the Law.

> Verses 4-25 – In an extensive campaign, Josiah eliminated every place of idolatrous worship, every idolatrous practice, and every idolatrous leader in the country. When his campaign reached to Bethel, he discovered the graves of the man of God who had prophesied his cleansing and the prophet who had caused him to disobey God by returning to the city.

> Verses 26-27 – Apparently, the repentance and reformation was only in the heart of the king – not in the spirit of the people – because God did not turn from His wrath against the idolatrous nation.

> Verses 28-30 – Josiah was killed in an invasion by the Egyptian king Necho.

> Verses 31-37 – Jehoahaz, who had succeeded his father as king, reigned only three months until Necho imprisoned him and took him to Egypt. Necho then placed Josiah's son Eliakim, whom he renamed Jehoiakim, on the throne and imposed a heavy tax upon the people. It is significant that both these kings are noted as having done evil in the sight of the Lord; the revival in their father's heart had not been conveyed to theirs.

Prayer Focus: Lord, I pray for revival, not just reform, to burn in our churches and to sweep our nation. Amen.
Notes:

Spiritual Journal:

Week: Thirty
Day: Thursday
Book: II Kings
Chapter: Twenty-four
Memory Verse: Twenty

Principle: Although the message of the whole Bible is that of the mercy and forgiveness of the Lord, it does contain the truth that there is a time in which the Lord will unleash His anger against those who do not keep His covenant. In Psalm 103:8-18 we read, *The LORD is merciful and gracious, slow to anger, and plenteous in mercy. He will not always chide: neither will he keep his anger for ever. He hath not dealt with us after our sins; nor rewarded us according to our iniquities. For as the heaven is high above the earth, so great is his mercy toward them that fear him. As far as the east is from the west, so far hath he removed our transgressions from us. Like as a father pitieth his children, so the LORD pitieth them that fear him. For he knoweth our frame; he remembereth that we are dust. As for man, his days are as grass: as a flower of the field, so he flourisheth. For the wind passeth over it, and it is gone; and the place thereof shall know it no more. But the mercy of the LORD is from everlasting to everlasting upon them that fear him, and his righteousness unto children's children; To such as keep his covenant, and to those that remember his commandments to do them.*

Outline:

Verses 1-7 – Because of their sins, God allowed Judah to be overrun by a host of their enemies, including the Babylonians, the Syrians, the Moabites, and the Ammonites.

Verses 8-16 – During Jehoiachin's reign, Nebuchadnezzar took captive the royal family and all the educated class of society and took them, along with all the remaining treasures of Judah, to Babylon.

Verses 17-20 – Zedekiah, Jehoiachin's uncle who was placed on the throne by Nebuchadnezzar, continued in the sinful ways of leadership of his predecessor.

Prayer Focus: Lord, help me to live in Your covenant blessing rather than to fall under Your judgment. Amen.

Notes:

Spiritual Journal:

Week: Thirty
Day: Friday
Book: II Kings
Chapter: Twenty-five
Memory Verse: Three
Principle: God's judgment is as exacting as His mercy is broad.
Outline:

    Verses 1-21 – After two years of siege against the city of Jerusalem, the Babylonians destroyed the city wall and burned the Temple, the important residences, and all the significant buildings. They killed the king's family while he watched and then blinded him. After taking all the artifacts left in the Temple, they carted away the bronze pillars that stood outside the entrance. Then they rounded up all the remaining men of influence and took them to Nebuchadnezzar, who had them killed.

    Verses 22-26 – Those who remained in the land were placed under the authority of a Babylonian governor who promised that they could live peacefully if they would submit to his government. Instead, the people assassinated him and all his associates – Jewish as well as Babylonian – and took refuge in Egypt.

    Verses 27-30 – After thirty-seven years of captivity, Jehoiachin was released from prison and given a position of respect in Babylon.

Prayer Focus: Lord, help me never to invoke Your wrath. Amen.
Notes:

Spiritual Journal:

Week: Thirty-one
Day: Monday
Book: I Chronicles
Chapter: One
Memory Verse: One
Principle: None of us are permanent here on earth. We all must face the realization that we are only visitors on this planet. As we come and go, we must leave our mark for future generations. We must realize that there is an interconnection throughout the entire human family and that we are all part of one another.
Outline:
Verses 1-28 – The family tree of Adam is given.
Verses 29-31 – Ishmael's family lineage is given.
Verses 32-33 – Abraham's descendants through his concubine Keturah are listed.
Verses 34-37 – Isaac's family is listed.
Verses 38-42 – The descendants of Seir (related to Esau) are listed.
Verses 43-54 – The kings of Edom (Seir) are given.
Prayer Focus: Lord, help me to never live for myself, but to always realize my part in Your universal family. Amen.
Notes:

Spiritual Journal:

Week: Thirty-one

Day: Tuesday

Book: I Chronicles

Chapter: Two

Memory Verses: One and two

Principle: Because so much – both good and bad – is transferred from parents to children, it is important to understand one's family roots and heritage.

Outline:

Verses 1-2 – Israel's family is listed.

Verses 3-17 – The lineage from Judah to David is traced.

Verses 18-24 – Hezron's family tree is given.

Verses 25-41 – Jerahmeel's heritage is spelled out.

Verses 42-55 – The history of Caleb's family is traced.

Prayer Focus: Lord, help me to be a vital link in transmitting to a new generation the good heritage I have received from the previous generations. Help me to be the termination point in transmission of any evil heritage that may be in my family tree. Amen.

Notes:

Spiritual Journal:

Week: Thirty-one
Day: Wednesday
Book: I Chronicles
Chapter: Three
Memory Verse: Nine

Principle: In the days of the Old Testament, keeping concubines was a totally legal and accepted practice; however, God had a different viewpoint. Notice that, although He acknowledged David's sons by his concubines, He did not list their names. We must remember the New Testament teaching about building our lives with enduring materials such as gold, silver, and precious stones rather than such readily degradable materials as wood, hay, and stubble.(I Corinthians 3:11-15)

Outline:
> Verses 1-9 – David's lineage is given.
> Verses 10-16 – Solomon's descendants are listed.
> Verses 17-24 – Jeconiah's family tree is given.

Prayer Focus: Lord, help me never to do anything that is simply good when You are calling me to do what is best. Help me never to settle for what is accepted and legal when You are calling me to what is righteous in Your eyes so that my life will leave an enduring heritage. Amen.

Notes:

Spiritual Journal:

Week: Thirty-one
Day: Thursday
Book: I Chronicles
Chapter: Four
Memory Verse: Ten
Principle: The New Testament teaches us that we do not have some of the blessings of
      God because we do not ask for them. Although Jabez had been marked from birth
      with a name which meant "pain," he decided to turn his destiny around by asking
      God to bless him and to keep him from causing anyone pain. Because of his faith
      and courage when he asked, he received everything he had requested from God.
Outline:
      Verses 1-23 – Judah's family tree is given.
      Verses 24-43 – Simeon's lineage is traced.
Prayer Focus: Lord, bless me indeed, enlarge my territory, let Your hand be with me, and
      keep me from evil, that I may not cause anyone pain! Amen.
Notes:

Spiritual Journal:

Week: Thirty-one
Day: Friday
Book: I Chronicles
Chapter: Five
Memory Verse: One
Principle: Although God is sovereign; He does not impose His will upon us. If we choose to disobey, the destinies that He had preordained for us are aborted by the actions of our own free will.
Outline:

Verses 1-10 – Reuben's lineage and some of their accomplishments are listed.

Verses 11-22 – The family of Gad is given, along with the fact that they were successful because they prayed to God for His help.

Verses 23-26 – The failures in the family of Manasseh are attributed to their unfaithfulness to the Lord.

Prayer Focus: Lord, help me to be obedient and to fulfill the destiny You have preplanned for me. Amen.

Notes:

Spiritual Journal:

Week: Thirty-two

Day: Monday

Book: I Chronicles

Chapter: Six

Memory Verse: Forty-nine

Principle: Godliness and dedication to God's service can be a family heritage. In Genesis, we read that God commanded all living things to produce after their own kind. In the history of Israel and throughout the history of the church, we can see many godly families that produce many great men and women of God.

Outline:

Verses 1-30 – The family tree of Levi is traced.

Verses 31-48 – The musicians in Levi's family are listed.

Verses 49-53 – Aaron's lineage is given.

Verses 54-81 – The dwelling places of the Levites are given.

Prayer Focus: Lord, help me to establish a legacy of faith and godliness as my family heritage. This is what I desire for my descendants to inherit from me. Amen.

Notes:

Spiritual Journal:

Week: Thirty-two
Day: Tuesday
Book: I Chronicles
Chapter: Seven
Memory Verse: Forty
Principle: *Lo, children are an heritage of the LORD: and the fruit of the womb is his reward. As arrows are in the hand of a mighty man; so are the children of his youth. Happy is the man that hath his quiver full of them: they shall not be ashamed, but they shall speak with their enemies in the gate.* (Psalm 127:3-5)
Outline:
       Verses 1-5 – Issachar's family was marked with men of great valor.
       Verses 6-12 – Benjamin's family were also men of great prowess.
       Verse 13 – Naphtali's sons are listed.
       Verses 14-19 – Manasseh's family tree through his concubine is added to the descendants listed in chapter five.
       Verses 20-29 – Ephraim's family endured losses as well as victories and increase.
       Verses 30-40 – Asher's family produced brave leaders.
Prayer Focus: Lord, I ask that my family be marked with great men and women who benefit the societies in which they live. Amen.
Notes:

Spiritual Journal:

Week: Thirty-two
Day: Wednesday
Book: I Chronicles
Chapter: Eight
Memory Verse: Forty
Principle: Though families may have their failures (as we saw in the life of King Saul), the blessings of God can be invoked (as we saw in the life of Jonathan) to overrule and bring ultimate blessing upon their heirs (as we see in today's verse).
Outline:
Verses 1-40 – The family tree of Benjamin, with focus on the family of King Saul, is traced.
Prayer Focus: Lord, help me to overcome any curse upon my family and to establish a heritage of blessing for my descendants. Amen.
Notes:

Spiritual Journal:

Week: Thirty-two
Day: Thursday
Book: I Chronicles
Chapter: Nine
Memory Verse: Thirty-four
Principle: The most important thing in our lives is to serve the Lord. We should become noteable for that one thing above all our other accomplishments.
Outline:

Verses 1-16 – A listing is given of those who lived in Jerusalem. Notable among them are the ones who served in the Temple.

Verses 17-27 – The Levites had the responsibility of keeping the gates to the Temple; therefore, they lived very close to the house of the Lord.

Verses 28-34 – Other responsibilities of the Levites are listed.

Verses 35-44 – The immediate family tree of King Saul is given.

Prayer Focus: Lord, help me always to remember and live by the little rhyme:

Only one life will soon be past.

Only what's done for Christ will last.

Amen.

Notes:

Spiritual Journal:

Week: Thirty-two
Day: Friday
Book: I Chronicles
Chapter: Ten
Memory Verse: Thirteen
Principle: There is always a day of reckoning for our sinful disobedience against God.
Outline:

        Verses 1-7 – King Saul suffered a tragic end when he committed suicide to escape being taken by his enemy; his three sons also died with him.

        Verses 8-10 – When the Philistines discovered the body of King Saul, they cut off his head and took it, along with his armor, to display in the temples of their pagan gods as a sign of their victory and a humiliation of the Israelites.

        Verses 11-12 – The brave men of Jabesh Gilead retrieved the bodies of the fallen king and his sons and gave them a proper burial accompanied by a seven-day fast.

        Verses 13-14 – God declares that Saul's demise was a direct result of his disobedience and involvement with witchcraft.

Prayer Focus: Lord, help me to always be sensitive to the fact that I will eventually pay for every sin unless I accept the payment You made for it on Calvary. Amen.

Notes:

Spiritual Journal:

Week: Thirty-three

Day: Monday

Book: I Chronicles

Chapter: Eleven

Memory Verse: Three

Principle: It is through faith and patience that we inherit the promises of God. (Hebrews 6:12, 10:36) David faithfully and loyally served Saul as he waited many years for the fulfillment of Samuel's promise that he was to be the next king.

Outline:

Verses 1-3 – The leaders of Israel voluntarily assembled and proclaimed David as their king.

Verses 4-9 – David took the Jebusite city of Jerusalem as his residence and the seat of his government.

Verses 10-47 – The men who served under David's rule became mighty men of valor with remarkable accomplishments to their credit.

Prayer Focus: Lord, help me to patiently wait in faith for You to fulfill Your promises to me. Amen.

Notes:

Spiritual Journal:

Week: Thirty-three
Day: Tuesday
Book: I Chronicles
Chapter: Twelve
Memory Verse: Eleven
Principle: God will always draw supporters to us in our time of need.
Outline:

      Verses 1-22 – God sent a steady stream of valiant men – as individuals and as groups – into David's camp.

      Verses 23-40 – His support grew to thousands from all the tribes of the land.

Prayer Focus: Lord, help me always to be aware of the supporters You send into my life and to be equally sensitive to Your leading when You are directing me to be someone's supporter.

Notes:

Spiritual Journal:

Week: Thirty-three
Day: Wednesday
Book: I Chronicles
Chapter: Thirteen
Memory Verse: Ten
Principle: We must not only follow our hearts when serving the Lord; we must also follow the instructions He has given to us in His Word.

Outline:

Verses 1-12 – David was inspired to bring the Ark of the Covenant to Jerusalem. Bringing the Ark to his new capital was certainly a noble thing to do. Because of David's desire to inquire of the Lord before the ark, we can only conclude that the plan was birthed out of his spiritual desire to serve the Lord. However, David erred in using the Philistines' method of transporting the Ark (I Samuel 6:8) rather than following the scriptural mandate that it be carried on the shoulders of the priests of God (Exodus 25:14). Because of David's negligence to carefully study and follow the written commandments of the Lord, one of his servants died needlessly.

Verses 13-14 – To prove that the curse David experienced was due to his disobedience rather than to the presence of the Ark itself, God brought blessings upon the household of Obed-Edom where the Ark was sheltered.

Prayer Focus: Lord, not only help me to follow the inspiration of my heart as I serve You, but help me to also apply my God-given intelligence to study Your written Word so that I can follow Your instructions. Amen.

Notes:

Spiritual Journal:

Week: Thirty-three
Day: Thursday
Book: I Chronicles
Chapter: Fourteen
Memory Verse: Ten
Principle: *Trust in the LORD with all thine heart; and lean not unto thine own understanding. In all thy ways acknowledge him, and he shall direct thy paths.* (Proverbs 3:5-6)
Outline:

> Verses 1-2 – The king of Tyre acknowledged David as the established king over Israel.
>
> Verses 3-7 – David took more wives and fathered more children after locating in Jerusalem.
>
> Verses 8-17 – When the Philistines came against Israel, David always inquired of the Lord whether he would be successful in fighting against them. The Lord answered by not only assuring him of victory but also giving him the strategy for the battle.

Prayer Focus: Lord, help me always to rely upon You rather than to take matters into my own hands and try to handle them with my own wisdom or resources. Amen.
Notes:

Spiritual Journal:

Week: Thirty-three

Day: Friday

Book: I Chronicles

Chapter: Fifteen

Memory Verse: Fifteen

Principle: After we have tragically erred or sinned, it is necessary to correct our ways and do things according to God's directives.

Outline:

Verses 1-29 – After the ill-fated attempt to bring the Ark of the Covenant to Jerusalem, David made a second attempt; this time, he followed God's commandment concerning proper handling of the Ark. The result was a jubilant entry into his new capital with the Ark borne on the shoulders of the appointed Levites.

Prayer Focus: Lord, grant me the wisdom, courage, and humility it takes to admit when I have erred and to correct my ways. Amen.

Notes:

Spiritual Journal:

Week: Thirty-four

Day: Monday

Book: I Chronicles

Chapter: Sixteen

Memory Verse: Twenty-four

Principle: In addition to our praises, worship, and offerings that God deserves, it is our obligation to proclaim Him among those who do not know that He is the Lord of the universe.

Outline:

Verses 1-6 – David held a great festival to celebrate the arrival of the Ark in Jerusalem. He then appointed the Levites, who were to care for the Ark and worship the Lord before it.

Verses 7-36 – David composed a psalm of praise to the Lord including explanations of how and why we are to worship Him:

a) His marvelous acts are to be proclaimed before the nations.

b) We are chosen by Him as targets of His goodness.

c) His covenants are established forever.

d) He established Israel and protected her among the hostile nations.

e) He is above all the idols that men proclaim to be gods.

f) Men must bring offerings and praise to the Lord.

g) Nature, as well, praises Him.

h) In our praise, we can also invoke His blessing and protection.

Verses 37-43 – Certain families were appointed to present sacrifices to God before the Ark, to sing praises to the Lord around the Ark, and to keep watch at the gates leading to the presence of the Ark.

Prayer Focus: Lord, help me always to have the devotion to praise You privately and the courage to praise You publicly. Amen.

Notes:

Spiritual Journal:

Week: Thirty-four
Day: Tuesday
Book: I Chronicles
Chapter: Seventeen
Memory Verse: Nineteen
Principle: It is God's good pleasure to bless His servants.
Outline:

Verses 1-15 – When David desired to build a Temple to house the Ark of the Covenant, his counselor Nathan originally encouraged him in his plan; however, the Lord spoke to the prophet that he had to correct his advice to the king. God said that rather than having David build a house (permanent building) for Him, He would build a house (dynasty) for David.

Verses 16-27 – David marveled at the graciousness of God in that He had already established the unknown shepherd boy in the position of king, and now – rather than accepting David's attempt to offer something to Him – the Lord was promising even more blessings to him. With amazement and gratitude, David accepted the Lord's blessings for the nation, himself, and his family.

Prayer Focus: Lord, thank You for Your loving care that always exceeds even my grandest imaginations. Amen.

Notes:

Spiritual Journal:

Week: Thirty-four

Day: Wednesday

Book: I Chronicles

Chapter: Eighteen

Memory Verse: Thirteen

Principle: To truly grasp today's principle, we must consider verse eleven as well as our chosen meditation verse. In verse eleven, we see that David dedicated to the Lord all the tribute that he received from Edom; verse thirteen tells us that the Lord preserved him as he established garrisons in Edom. The Lord will preserve and establish us in any area of our lives that we will dedicate to Him.

Outline:

Verses 1-13 – David's great successes and the expansion of his territory, influence, and wealth are attributed to his dedication to the Lord.

Verses 14-17 – David established choice men in positions of leadership to assist him in administering judgment and justice to the people.

Prayer Focus: Lord, help me to always acknowledge You in every area of my life so that You can establish my paths. Amen.

Notes:

Spiritual Journal:

Week: Thirty-four
Day: Thursday
Book: I Chronicles
Chapter: Nineteen
Memory Verse: Thirteen
Principle: It is favorable in the Lord's sight to do what brings benefit to His children.
Outline:

Verses 1-3 – David's act of condolence toward Hanun at the death of his father was misconstrued as an attempt to spy out any possible weaknesses of the Ammonites.

Verses 4-7 – After Hanun humiliated David's envoy, he realized that he had stirred up trouble for himself, so he hired Syrian mercenaries to help protect his nation from David's retaliation.

Verses 8-19 – Discovering that his army was sandwiched between the Ammonites and the Syrians, Joab split his forces into two groups – one under his command and one under the command of Abishai – to fight the two opponents. After pledging themselves to bravery and calling upon the Lord's favor, they defeated both enemies with great triumph.

Prayer Focus: Lord, help me always to trust that You have my best interest in mind and that it is actually pleasurable to You to give me the benefits of Your kingdom. Amen.

Notes:

Spiritual Journal:

Week: Thirty-four
Day: Friday
Book: I Chronicles
Chapter: Twenty
Memory Verse: Eight
Principle: David went out against Goliath with five stones because he knew that he would eventually have to defeat his four brothers as well. We must also be intent on seeing every commission from God all the way through to completion.
Outline:

Verses 1-3 – The defeat of the Ammonites brought great wealth to David's kingdom.

Verses 4-8 – In various conflicts with the Philistines, David's mighty warriors encountered and slew the brothers of Goliath.

Prayer Focus: Lord, may my life be characterized by the same commitment that Jesus expressed when He said that His purpose was to do Your will and to finish Your work. (John 4:34) Amen.

Notes:

Spiritual Journal:

Week: Thirty-five
Day: Monday
Book: I Chronicles
Chapter: Twenty-one
Memory Verse: Thirteen
Principle: Our sins and errors often bring consequences that affect many innocent victims.
Outline:

Verses 1-6 – David's decision to take a census of the fighting men available to him was in direct contradiction to his statement of reliance upon God recorded in Psalm 20:7, *Some trust in chariots, and some in horses: but we will remember the name of the LORD our God.* When this section is compared with the recounting of the same event in II Samuel 24, we see that David was acting under the influence of Satan, who was apparently allowed to control David because the Lord's anger was against him. Even though David's top general advised him against the census, he insisted that it be taken. Joab was able to follow the orders given him yet stay true to his own conscience by not including all the tribes of the land when he took the count.

Verses 7-14 – When the Lord offered David three alternatives as his judgment, the king chose a three-day plague with the anticipation that the Lord would be more merciful than a human enemy.

Verses 15-18 – When the plague reached Jerusalem, David interceded and was directed to the location that later became the Temple Mount to make a sacrifice unto the Lord.

Verses 19-27 – When the owner of the property wanted to give the land to David without charge, David insisted that he was going to pay full price because it was to be his personal sacrifice to the Lord. As soon as the offering was made, the plague ended.

Verses 28-30 – Even though the tabernacle of Moses was in Gibeon, the threshing floor became David's place to intercede before the Lord because David still feared or respected the vengeance of the Lord.

Prayer Focus: Lord, help me to live uprightly, realizing how my failures will affect me and also have fallout in the lives of others. Amen.
Notes:

Spiritual Journal:

Week: Thirty-five

Day: Tuesday

Book: I Chronicles

Chapter: Twenty-two

Memory Verse: Thirteen

Principle: No matter how great the task before us may be, we can accomplish it if we honor and obey the Lord and act with divinely inspired courage.

Outline:

> Verses 1-5 – Even though David knew that it would not be his task or privilege to build the house of the Lord, he amassed a great wealth of materials and gathered a massive work force in preparation for the project that his son would undertake.

> Verses 6-16 – King David called his son Solomon and explained to him that the privilege and responsibility of building the Temple was to be his. He explained to him that the materials and workers for the great project were already in place. The one thing lacking was the leader to undertake the project. David further explained that Solomon needed wisdom from the Lord to accomplish the task. Such divine wisdom would only come through Solomon's determined obedience to the commandments of the Lord and his fearless courage.

> Verses 17-19 – The king then called the leaders of the nation and charged them to unite with Solomon in this massive project.

Prayer Focus: Lord, help me never to shrink back from any assignment You set before me. Help me, rather, to tackle and accomplish each challenge with a heart of obedience and an attitude of courage. Amen.

Notes:

Spiritual Journal:

Week: Thirty-five
Day: Wednesday
Book: I Chronicles
Chapter: Twenty-three
Memory Verse: Thirty
Principle: Our praise to the Lord should not be limited to Sunday worship but should be a
daily part of our lives.
Outline:
Verses 1-24 – The tribe of Levi was especially separated unto the Lord to serve in
the formal duties of the sacrifice system and Temple worship.
Verses 25-32 – Now that a permanent Temple was to be erected as Israel's place
of worship rather than the traveling tabernacle, many of the duties of the
Levites had to be reassigned.
Prayer Focus: Lord, help me to set aside daily times of formal worship and always keep
my heart open for moments of informal impromptu worship and fellowship with
You. Amen.
Notes:

Spiritual Journal:

Week: Thirty-five

Day: Thursday

Book: I Chronicles

Chapter: Twenty-four

Memory Verse: Three

Principle: Every person has a part to play in fulfilling the ministry of the church to the world and before God. In the New Testament, the church is called the Body of Christ and is likened unto the human body with many members, each one serving in its own way to fulfill its unique role in the overall ministry in God's kingdom.

Outline:

Verses 1-19 – King David and Zadok, the chief priest, cast lots to divide the Temple responsibilities among the members of the priestly family and to establish their rotation in fulfilling these duties.

Verses 20-31 – The responsibilities and rotation schedule of the Levites were also established by casting lots.

Prayer Focus: Lord, help me to never belittle or exalt my individual role in Your kingdom. Help me to always fulfill my part of the ministry to the fullest of the ability You have placed within me, with all the zeal I can muster, and with the highest possible level of cooperation and respect for all the other members of Your body as we work together for one common goal. Amen.

Notes:

Spiritual Journal:

Week: Thirty-five

Day: Friday

Book: I Chronicles

Chapter: Twenty-five

Memory Verse: Seven

Principle: The scriptures are abundantly clear that music is a vital part of true worship unto the Lord. According to Psalm 100:2, it is through singing that we are able to enter into His presence.

Outline:

Verses 1-31 – David took special care to appoint skillful, anointed men to serve as musicians before the Lord during the Temple worship.

Prayer Focus: Lord, release my spirit man to sing joyfully before You continually. Amen.

Notes:

Spiritual Journal:

Week: Thirty-six
Day: Monday
Book: I Chronicles
Chapter: Twenty-six
Memory Verse: Six
Principle: God deserves and wants our best abilities to be employed in our service unto
and before Him.
Outline:
Verses 1-19 – Certain families were appointed to keep the gates of the Temple.
Verses 20-32 – Other families were given the responsibility of guarding the
treasures that were stored in the Temple.
Prayer Focus: Lord, help me to give nothing less than my best in Your service. Amen.
Notes:

Spiritual Journal:

Week: Thirty-six
Day: Tuesday
Book: I Chronicles
Chapter: Twenty-seven
Memory Verse: One
Principle: Every person has a divine purpose to fulfill and fits into God's orderly plan.
Outline:

> Verses 1-15 – The military positions and responsibilities were organized under David's supervision.
>
> Verses 16-24 – The leadership within the tribes of Israel also had a systematic division and organization.
>
> Verses 25-34 – Methodical arrangements were made for taking care of all the agricultural assignments within the kingdom.

Prayer Focus: Lord, help me to recognize my individual role in the kingdom of God and to understand how I must fit into the overall scheme that You have set in place in Your divine economy. Amen.

Notes:

Spiritual Journal:

Week: Thirty-six
Day: Wednesday
Book: I Chronicles
Chapter: Twenty-eight
Memory Verse: Twenty

Principle: God has promised – and actually already supplied – all we ever need in order to fulfill our commissions and assignments; all we need is the courage to act in faith, believing that He will make good on His promises.

Outline:

Verses 1-19 – David called a public assembly in which he commissioned his son Solomon to build the Temple. He explained how it had been on his heart to build the Temple himself but that God had directed him that it would be his son who would fulfill the assignment. David explained how he had made all the necessary arrangements in terms of recording the plans that had been given him by the Holy Spirit, collecting the necessary materials, and arranging the talented workers for the project. The two things Solomon needed were an intimate relationship with God (verse 9) and the bold faith to trust God as he acted upon his commission (verse 20).

Prayer Focus: Lord, today I pray as the author of Hebrews admonished us that I not fail to enter into Your provisions because of a lack of bold faith to trust You and act upon Your promises. Amen.

Notes:

Spiritual Journal:

Week: Thirty-six

Day: Thursday

Book: I Chronicles

Chapter: Twenty-nine

Memory Verse: Twenty

Principle: In this closing chapter of David's life, we see a magnificent culmination to many of the great qualities that marked his life and brought him such great success: dedication, sincerity, thankfulness, sacrifice, dependence, planning, and humility.

Outline:

Verses 1-9 – When David passed his vision on to the leadership of Israel, they caught onto his zeal and also gave sacrificially for the Temple's expenses.

Verses 10-15 – With humility, David expressed his praise and thanksgiving unto the Lord.

Verses 16-20 – He expressed a transparency in his worship before the Lord and led his people into that same openness before Him.

Verses 21-25 – Solomon was enthroned in the place of his father.

Verses 26-30 – David's death ended forty years of noble leadership.

Prayer Focus: Lord, may I continue to live by Your great principles and bear good fruit until the very last day of my earthly assignment. Amen.

Notes:

Spiritual Journal:

Week: Thirty-six
Day: Friday
Book: II Chronicles
Chapter: One
Memory Verse: One
Principle: All true success is because of the Lord's promotion, not because of our human abilities or achievements. (Psalm 75:6)
Outline:

> Verses 1-6 – Solomon initiated his reign by making a magnificent display of his dedication to and dependence upon the Lord.
>
> Verses 7-12 – When the Lord appeared to Solomon and promised to grant him the desire of his heart, the new king asked for wisdom to rule the nation. Pleased by the unselfishness of this request, the Lord proclaimed that Solomon would indeed have the wisdom he desired but would also receive all the material blessings and prosperity that he could have requested.
>
> Verses 13-17 – Solomon's reign was marked by the influx of great wealth to Israel.

Prayer Focus: Lord, help me to remember and live by the words penned by this great man of history: *Wisdom is the principal thing; therefore get wisdom: and with all thy getting get understanding.* (Proverbs 4:7)

Notes:

Spiritual Journal:

Week: Thirty-seven
Day: Monday
Book: II Chronicles
Chapter: Two
Memory Verse: Six
Principle: It is vitally important to keep a proper perspective on the magnificence of God lest we over-evaluate our significance or the import of our accomplishments.
Outline:
Verses 1-10 – Solomon petitioned Hiram, king of Tyre, to provide supplies and craftsmen to assist in the Temple project.
Verses 11-16 – Hiram graciously acknowledged Solomon and generously promised to oblige him with his requests.
Verses 17-18 – Solomon conscripted all the foreigners in the land to work on his construction project.
Prayer Focus: Lord, help me never to get my focus on myself, my problems, my accomplishments, or my failures – and lose sight of You and Your magnificence. Amen.
Notes:

Spiritual Journal:

Week: Thirty-seven
Day: Tuesday
Book: II Chronicles
Chapter: Three
Memory Verse: Six
Principle: We should give our very best in our labors for the Lord.
Outline:

Verses 1-17 – Solomon barred no expenses in his construction of the Temple; he undertook it on a grand scale with lavish generosity. The main building was ninety feet by thirty feet and the entranceway was thirty feet by thirty and thirty feet (some versions suggest one hundred seventy feet) high. Much of this was overlaid with gold and precious stones. The Most Holy Place was thirty feet by thirty feet and was overlaid with 114,000 pounds of pure gold. The golden cherubim who stood over the Ark of the Covenant had a combined wingspan of thirty feet. The bronze pillars before the sanctuary stood at twenty-seven (some records suggest fifty-three) feet tall.

Prayer Focus: Lord, may I never be "chintzy" or "cheap" – in other words, selfish and faithless – when I attempt things for Your kingdom. Amen.

Notes:

Spiritual Journal:

Week: Thirty-seven
Day: Wednesday
Book: II Chronicles
Chapter: Four
Memory Verse: Eighteen
Principle: In our giving to the Lord, it is sometimes necessary to become so open-hearted and open-handed that we fail to keep account of our generosity.
Outline:
> Verses 1-22 – Solomon furnished the Temple so extravagantly that he lost count of the quantity of materials used in producing the golden implements and bronze fixtures. One example of the magnitude of the project can be seen in the brazen sea which held over eight thousand gallons of water.

Prayer Focus: Lord, help me to understand and live by the balance between being a good steward who keeps accurate record of the resources entrusted to him and exhibiting faithful generosity which takes me to the point that *the right hand doesn't know what the left one is doing.* (Matthew 6:3) Amen.

Notes:

Spiritual Journal:

Week: Thirty-seven
Day: Thursday
Book: II Chronicles
Chapter: Five
Memory Verse: Thirteen
Principle: When believers become united with their total focus on worshipping the Lord,
He will manifest Himself mightily to them, through them, in them, and for them.
Outline:
Verses 1-3 – When the construction and furnishing of the Temple was completed,
Solomon called a nationwide celebration for its dedication.
Verses 4-10 – The placing of the Ark of the Covenant in the Most Holy Place was
the zenith of the celebration, marked by innumerable sacrifices. The fact
that the poles of the Ark were visible beyond the curtain that kept the Ark
itself from view gave the people an assurance that the Ark was present
even though they could not see it. It is likely that this was done as a
symbol of faith, which is defined as the substance of things we hope for
and the evidence of things that we do not see.
Verses 11-14 – When the priests and Levites who had sanctified themselves for
this momentous occasion joined in unified worship to the Lord, they were
so overwhelmed by the presence of the Holy Spirit, which manifested in a
cloud, that they were unable to continue with their assigned duties.
Prayer Focus: Lord, I desire to have my natural life interrupted and overruled as it was
here and on the Day of Pentecost, but I realize from the stories of each of these
divine visitations that they must be preceded by a total unity within Your body
and a concentrated focus on You. Therefore, in my prayer today I echo Jesus'
request as recorded in John chapter seventeen – that the church may be one as the
divine Trinity are one. Amen.
Notes:

Spiritual Journal:

Week: Thirty-seven
Day: Friday
Book: II Chronicles
Chapter: Six
Memory Verse: Thirty-nine

Principle: Even though Solomon had built a magnificent sanctuary for the Lord, he acknowledged that his own works were not sufficient for salvation as he repeatedly asked God to hear from heaven – not the Temple – and to forgive and heal His people. We too must realize that it is the humbleness and brokenness of our hearts – not our works – that God desires.

Outline:

Verses 1-11 – Solomon recounted the covenant that the Lord had initiated with King David and testified to the Lord's faithfulness in fulfilling His Word.

Verses 12-17 – Solomon interceded for the covenant to be renewed with his own rule in Israel.

Verses 18-42 – With an acknowledgment that the very heaven of heavens could not contain the full presence of the Lord, Solomon recognized the inadequacy of the Temple he had built. He then declared the true significance of the place by repeatedly asking that it serve as a focal or contact point for the people's intercession.

Prayer Focus: Lord, help me never to forget that nothing I can do other than honest repentance and simple faith will ever be adequate to meet Your standards. Amen.

Notes:

Spiritual Journal:

Week: Thirty-eight
Day: Monday
Book: II Chronicles
Chapter: Seven
Memory Verse: Fourteen
Principle: The real key to having God's blessings in our lives is simple repentance and true humility before Him.
Outline:

Verses 1-11 – Solomon dedicated the Temple with an epic display of pageantry, celebration, feasting, and sacrifices. The zenith of this event came when God miraculously sent heavenly fire to consume the sacrifices and visible glory to fill the Temple.

Verses 12-22 – The Lord appeared to Solomon and renewed the covenant with him affirming that the royal lineage (the house of David) and the Temple (the house of God) would remain as long as the people would serve Him. He further promised to forgive and restore the people any time they sincerely repented; however, He also warned that, if they turned from serving the Lord, they would be expelled from the Promised Land, the Temple would come to ruin, and the people would experience such severe judgment that they would become a byword, or public example, among the other nations.

Prayer Focus: Lord, as I call upon You with repentance and humbling myself, I ask You to hear my cry and respond with forgiveness and healing. Amen.

Notes:

Spiritual Journal:

Week: Thirty-eight

Day: Tuesday

Book: II Chronicles

Chapter: Eight

Memory Verse: Sixteen

Principle: Many people fail because they do not set goals and develop strategies to achieve those goals. The unfortunate thing is that many of these people blame their lack of achievement on not having had a commandment or a direction from the Lord concerning what they were supposed to do with their lives.

Outline:

Verses 1-6 – During the first twenty years of his reign, Solomon accomplished almost unimaginable achievements in the expansion and development of Israel's territories.

Verses 7-10 – His accomplishments were possible because he had a carefully laid out plan of operation and an understanding of how to best utilize the resources and work force available to him.

Verses 11-15 – The greatest key to Solomon's success was his piety and reverence for the Lord, which was demonstrated in the fact that he was careful not to desecrate the holy city by allowing his pagan wife to live there and by his careful preparation for and observance of the details of the Temple worship ceremony and ritual.

Verse 16 – Because he had a carefully worked out plan that he followed through to completion, Solomon was able to accomplish his goal of building the magnificent Temple to the Lord.

Verses 17-18 – Another significant factor in Solomon's planning was the institution of a financial program by which he secured the wealth necessary to fund his visionary project.

Prayer Focus: Lord, direct me as I plan my work and empower me as I work my plan. Amen.

Notes:

Spiritual Journal:

Week: Thirty-eight
Day: Wednesday
Book: II Chronicles
Chapter: Nine
Memory Verse: Six
Principle: God is the God who does more than we would ever think or ask. (Ephesians
        3:20)
Outline:
        Verses 1-12 – When the queen of Sheba came to Jerusalem to investigate what
           she had supposed were exaggerated reports about Solomon's exceeding
           wealth and wisdom, she was overwhelmed and actually fainted at what she
           found: splendor and wisdom which far exceeded her expectations and all
           that had been told her.
        Verses 13-24 – Solomon's great wealth is characterized by his annual
           procurement of 126,000 pounds of gold, which he used lavishly in
           decorating the Temple and his throne room.
        Verses 25-26 – His military superiority is characterized by his extensive cavalry
           of twelve thousand horses and four thousand stalls to house those horses
           and chariots.
        Verses 27-31 – During his forty-year reign, Solomon raised the standard of living
           in Jerusalem so extensively that silver became as common as stones.
Prayer Focus: Lord, because You are the God who so lavishly gives good gifts to Your
        children, help me not to be like the Israelites who limited the Holy One (Psalm
        78:41); let me, rather, live as William Carey once said, expecting great things
        from You while attempting great things for You. Amen.
Notes:

Spiritual Journal:

Week: Thirty-eight
Day: Thursday
Book: II Chronicles
Chapter: Ten
Memory Verse: Fifteen

Principle: Even in the most ungodly situations, God is at work behind the scenes. In Romans 13:1, Paul instructed us, *Let every soul be subject unto the higher powers. For there is no power but of God: the powers that be are ordained of God.* In this admonition, we are reminded that God is sovereign and that He will eventually manifest His plan and purpose through even the most diabolical men.

Outline:

Verses 1-4 – Jeroboam, who had sought refuge in Egypt during the reign of Solomon, returned to Israel at the coronation of Rehoboam as king in his father's place. He returned to champion the cause of the people who had been subject to heavy taxation under Solomon's administration.

Verses 5-14 – When Rehoboam took the demands presented by Jeroboam to the elders who had advised Solomon, they responded that the requests were reasonable and should be granted. The new king next presented the petition to the young men with whom he had grown up. Their advice, colored by their experience of having grown up with all the luxuries afforded to the ruling class at the expense of the common citizenry, was to reject the plea of the people and, instead, levy heavier taxation upon them.

Verses 15-17 – Even in his selfishness, lack of wisdom, and rebelliousness, Rehoboam was unknowingly acting according to God's prophetic plan to set up the conditions that precipitated the division of the kingdom into two separate nations.

Verses 18-19 – The division was consummated when the people stoned the tax collector and sent the king fleeing to Jerusalem for safety.

Prayer Focus: Lord, help me never to get my focus so much on the historic events which happen in the world around me that I fail to see the history You are orchestrating through them. Amen.

Notes & Spiritual Journal:

Week: Thirty-eight

Day: Friday

Book: II Chronicles

Chapter: Eleven

Memory Verse: Four

Principle: Listening to and following the Lord's instructions can save us from much conflict in our lives.

Outline:

        Verses 1-4 – When Rehoboam decided to use military force to bring the separated tribes back under his control, Shemaiah spoke out against the plan; the king wisely heeded the prophet's warning and canceled the campaign.

        Verses 5-12 – Rehoboam did, however, strongly fortify Judah by building military cities throughout his kingdom.

        Verses 13-17 – Jeroboam, who was promoting idolatry in Israel, put the Levites out of work. Along with the devoted men of the country who wanted to continue worshipping God, these religious leaders immigrated to Judah, where they helped Rehoboam lead the nation in the ways established by his father and grandfather.

        Verses 18-23 – Rehoboam took eighteen wives and sixty concubines who bore him twenty-eight sons and sixty daughters. He strategically placed his sons throughout the country to insure a royal presence in all areas of his domain.

Prayer Focus: Lord, grant me the wisdom to listen to Your advice and warnings before I act rather than having to hear Your corrections after my actions. Amen.

Notes:

Spiritual Journal:

Week: Thirty-nine
Day: Monday
Book: II Chronicles
Chapter: Twelve
Memory Verse: Twelve

Principle: Most of the hurtful things that occur in our lives can be avoided by simply living righteously before the Lord. The life of Rehoboam illustrated the divine principle that many of our difficulties should be considered as self-inflicted through our disobedience and that they can be remedied by simple repentance and humbling ourselves before the Lord. Psalm 34:19 tells us that the Lord delivers the righteous out of all his afflictions.

Outline:

Verses 1-4 – When Rehoboam turned from serving the Lord, the Egyptian king launched a massive military campaign against him.

Verses 5-12 – In response to the correction of God through His prophet, Rehoboam and the leaders of Judah humbled themselves before the Lord, resulting in their deliverance. Although the Lord stopped the Egyptians from totally overtaking the kingdom, the people of Judah did suffer a certain amount of injury at their hands – including the loss of the golden shields that Solomon had fashioned for the Temple. Rehoboam's response was to substitute brass shields for the lost golden ones.

Verses 13-16 – Even though we have been given the story of Rehoboam's repentance and his recovery, it is tragic to read the summary of his seventeen-year reign: *He did evil because he prepared not his heart to seek the LORD.* It is true that our mistakes and failures are often remembered long after our good deeds are forgotten.

Prayer Focus: Lord, thank you that You are gracious to restore me when I repent, but my desire is that I not have to endure a fall even though I have the promise of recovery; therefore, I pray today as You taught in the Lord's Prayer that I be delivered from evil and that I not be led into temptation. Amen.

Notes:

Spiritual Journal:

Week: Thirty-nine

Day: Tuesday

Book: II Chronicles

Chapter: Thirteen

Memory Verse: Eighteen

Principle: The Lord is our defense, our strong tower, and our deliverer. If we trust in Him, He will give us victory – even against formidable odds.

Outline:

Verses 1-3 – When Abijah and Jeroboam were drawn into battle, the army of Israel outnumbered the forces of Judah two-to-one.

Verses 4-12 – Abijah challenged Israel with the fact that, while they had broken the Davidic covenant and had followed false gods, Judah had remained faithful to the household of David and had continued to serve the Lord.

Verses 13-18 – Even though Jeroboam employed a potentially devastating battle strategy, the people of Judah cried unto the Lord, and He gave them a great victory.

Verses 19-20 – Not only did Judah win the present battle, they continued to subdue Israel and weaken them throughout the reign of Abijah.

Verses 21-22 – Abijah had fourteen wives, twenty-two sons, and sixteen daughters.

Prayer Focus: Lord, today I renew my determination to trust in You rather than any physical source of strength or defense. Amen.

Notes:

Spiritual Journal:

Week: Thirty-nine
Day: Wednesday
Book: II Chronicles
Chapter: Fourteen
Memory Verse: Eleven
Principle: When God is on our side – and we are on His side – no one can stand against
　　　us.
Outline:
　　　Verses 1-7 – After the death of his father Abijah, Asa took the throne of Judah.
　　　　　His reign was marked by peace with the surrounding countries and
　　　　　prosperity within the country. He brought about a sweeping reform in the
　　　　　land by removing the pagan worship and fortifying the cities.
　　　Verses 8-15 – When the king of Ethiopia attacked with a force roughly twice the
　　　　　strength of Asa's army, the king of Judah cried unto the Lord and declared
　　　　　his dependency upon Him. The Lord not only gave Judah victory over the
　　　　　attacking forces, He also delivered the wealth of the region of Gerar into
　　　　　their hand.
Prayer Focus: Lord, help me not to use my physical resources as my gauge, but to always
　　　place my confidence in You, knowing that You can – and will – deliver me
　　　whether by many or by few.(I Samuel 14:6) Amen.
Notes:

Spiritual Journal:

Week: Thirty-nine
Day: Thursday
Book: II Chronicles
Chapter: Fifteen
Memory Verse: Two
Principle: Success or failure, peace or turmoil, blessings or cursing – all these are choices
we make, not circumstances in which we find ourselves. The choice is simply our
decision to serve the Lord or to abandon Him in our daily lives and decisions.
Outline:
Verses 1-7 – The prophet Azariah confronted King Asa with an analysis of
history and the present and advised him concerning the future. After
pointing out that the kingdom was in peace and prosperity when they
served the Lord and that all nations and peoples suffered turmoil when
they abandoned Him, the prophet challenged the king to courageously
undertake bringing about a reform in the land.

Verses 8-19 – In his sweeping reform, Asa eradicated pagan idols and
worshippers throughout the land – even to the extent that he removed his
own mother from power because she reverenced a pagan image. As a
result of his bold stand for godliness, the righteous people from the
surrounding nations flocked to Judah to become part of the covenant
renewal, which was marked by a great celebration and the sacrifice of
seven hundred bulls and seven thousand sheep. He also greatly enriched
the Temple with silver and gold. Although he did not remove all the high
places where false religious practices were observed, God honored his zeal
and dedication by giving the nation peace throughout his reign.

Prayer Focus: Lord, may I constantly focus on godliness – not just so that I can have
Your approval – but simply because I love You! Amen.
Notes:

Spiritual Journal:

Week: Thirty-nine
Day: Friday
Book: II Chronicles
Chapter: Sixteen
Memory Verse: Nine
Principle: Contrary to how we often feel – that we need to try to beg or entice God to help us – the truth is that He is always looking for an opportunity to assist His people.
Outline:
    Verses 1-6 – When the king of Israel started to fortify the border to prevent the emigration of people from his kingdom into Judah, Asa invoked the assistance of Ben-Hadad. As a result of the Syrians' attack, Israel discontinued their work at Ramah, and Judah confiscated the building materials and used them to construct their own cities.

    Verses 7-10 – Hanani challenged Asa concerning his decision to seek Syria's assistance. Citing the example of how Judah had overcome the Ethiopians and the Lubim without outside help, the prophet reminded the king that, not only God Himself was on his side, He was actually looking for an occasion to help him! Asa, however, became so angered at Hanani's words that he had the prophet imprisoned.

    Verses 11-14 – Although Asa became seriously ill, he refused to call upon the Lord for healing and died as a result of his condition. The tragedy of the story is that his malady was not really the problem in his feet, but the one in his heart – because, even though he had started his reign with great dependence upon and loyalty to the Lord, he had turned away from his faith.

Prayer Focus: Lord, my greatest desire is that You may judge my heart as being perfect toward You. Amen.
Notes:

Spiritual Journal:

Week: Forty
Day: Monday
Book: II Chronicles
Chapter: Seventeen
Memory Verse: Nine
Principle: Studying and understanding the Word of the Lord is the key to a victorious life:

Thy word have I hid in mine heart, that I might not sin against thee. (Psalm 119:11) *Study to shew thyself approved unto God, a workman that needeth not to be ashamed, rightly dividing the word of truth.* (II Timothy 2:15) *All scripture is given by inspiration of God, and is profitable for doctrine, for reproof, for correction, for instruction in righteousness that the man of God may be perfect, throughly furnished unto all good works.* (II Timothy 3:16-17) *This book of the law shall not depart out of thy mouth; but thou shalt meditate therein day and night, that thou mayest observe to do according to all that is written therein: for then thou shalt make thy way prosperous, and then thou shalt have good success.* (Joshua 1:8)

Outline:

Verses 1-6 – When Jehoshaphat took the throne of his father Asa, he strengthened the nation both militarily and spiritually. The Lord established his rule because he delighted in the ways and laws of God.

Verses 7-9 – One of Jehoshaphat's wisest moves was to educate the people in the scripture.

Verses 10-13 – As Jehoshaphat increased in wealth and power, the neighboring countries brought tribute to show him honor.

Verses 14-19 – The mighty men who surrounded Jehoshaphat were well organized and full of valor.

Prayer Focus: Lord, today I dedicate myself anew to Your Word – both to know and follow it in my own life and to share it with whomever will allow me to teach them. Amen.

Notes:

Spiritual Journal:

Week: Forty
Day: Tuesday
Book: II Chronicles
Chapter: Eighteen
Memory Verse: Six
Principle: God is our only source of true information, instruction, counsel, and advice.
Outline:

  Verses 1-3 – In an attempt to unify the nation of Judah with the nation of Israel, Jehoshaphat, who had married into the royal family of the northern kingdom, agreed to go with them in battle against the Syrians.

  Verses 4-17 – At Jehoshaphat's request, Ahab called the prophets together to predict the outcome of the battle. Although all four hundred predicted victory, the king of Judah asked for a second opinion from one more prophet. Because the messenger who called him warned Micaiah that he should agree with the other prophets, he mockingly predicted victory. After being challenged by the king of Israel, Micaiah prophesied chaos and loss in the conflict.

  Verses 18-27 – After Micaiah explained that a lying spirit had been speaking through the other prophets in order to draw Ahab to his demise in the battle, the king was enraged and had the prophet thrown into prison.

  Verses 28-34 – Although Ahab disguised himself as he entered the battle and although the king of Syria had given strict orders that no one other than the king be attacked, a randomly shot arrow found the one vulnerable spot in the king's armor and struck a fatal blow against him.

Prayer Focus: Lord, I determine to not listen to ungodly counsel or depend upon my limited reasoning power; rather, I will wait to act until I have heard from You. Amen.

Notes:

Spiritual Journal:

Week: Forty

Day: Wednesday

Book: II Chronicles

Chapter: Nineteen

Memory Verse: Seven

Principle: As God's earthly representatives, we must live with courageous honesty and aggressive integrity.

Outline:

        Verses 1-3 – Although the prophet had to rebuke Jehoshaphat for allying with the wicked king of Israel, he also commended him for his righteous reign in Judah.

        Verses 4-13 – Jehoshaphat set righteous judges in position throughout the land and commissioned them to boldly fulfill their role of dispensing fair rulings and impartial decisions.

Prayer Focus: Lord, my prayer is that I may live up to the requirement that You have made of man in Micah 6:8 – to do justly, and to love mercy, and to walk humbly with You. Amen.

Notes:

Spiritual Journal:

Week: Forty

Day: Thursday

Book: II Chronicles

Chapter: Twenty

Memory Verse: Twenty-two

Principle: Praising God in the midst of our difficulties – rather than waiting until we have already had the victory – is proof of our faith. It shows God – and our enemy – that we believe in advance in God's deliverance. We have already experienced the deliverance in the faith realm, even before we have had the victory in the physical dimension.

Outline:

Verses 1-13 – When Jehoshaphat received the news that three armies had combined their forces to attack, he called a national day of intercession and covenant renewal.

Verses 14-19 – When the prophet proclaimed that Judah would be delivered without a fight, the king bowed in worship and the people rose in praise to the Lord for the promised victory.

Verses 20-23 – The musicians, whose job it was to lead the army home in a victory march *after* the battle, were commissioned to play *before* the fight as a declaration of faith in the promised deliverance. As they played, the enemy armies were so confused that they began to fight among themselves.

Verses 24-30 – Rather than engaging in conflict with the foe, the army of Judah simply marched onto the battlefield to collect the booty of the slain enemy.

Verses 31-36 – Although Jehoshaphat's reign was characterized by righteous reform, there was still idolatry at the grassroots level among the people. When the king himself resisted the warning of the prophet of God and unwisely aligned his kingdom with wicked Israel, their joint business ventures proved to be disastrous.

Prayer Focus: Lord, I determine to demonstrate my faith when I pray by following the Apostle Paul's advice to thank You even before I have physically received Your answer: *Be careful for nothing; but in every thing by prayer and supplication with thanksgiving let your requests be made known unto God.* (Philippians 4:6) Amen.

Notes & Spiritual Journal:

Week: Forty
Day: Friday
Book: II Chronicles
Chapter: Twenty-one
Memory Verse: Twenty

Principle: We must live our lives with constant view of our deaths. Our daily goal should be to build a legacy which will remain after we depart and to establish a place in society and the hearts of those around us so that when we pass on they will all realize that a little bit of heaven has gone home.

Outline:

Verses 1-7 – Jehoram, who ruled Judah for eight years after his father's death, murdered his brothers and all other possible contenders for the throne. He also married into the evil royal family of Israel and led Judah into the idolatry so common in the northern kingdom. Although his reign was marked with wickedness, the Lord did not destroy his household because of the covenant He had established with his forefather David.

Verses 8-11 – Because of the spiritual rebellion in Judah, the Edomites physically rebelled against their rule.

Verses 12-15 – The prophet Elijah warned Jehoram of the impending judgment from God because of his idolatry.

Verses 16-19 – Each statement in Elijah's prophecy was explicitly fulfilled as the king suffered external and internal attacks. Externally, the Philistines and Ethiopians attacked Judah and plundered Jehoram's wealth and captured or killed his wives and children – leaving only one young son in the kingdom. Internally, an incurable intestinal disease took his life.

Verse 20 – The tragic statement that summed up his life was that his death was to no one's sorrow.

Prayer Focus: Lord, may my life bring joy to others and my death leave a void in the world where I have lived. Amen.

Notes:

Spiritual Journal:

Week: Forty-one
Day: Monday
Book: II Chronicles
Chapter: Twenty-two
Memory Verse: Three
Principle: It is of ultimate importance that we are careful whose advice we receive. Wrong counsel can destroy our careers, our influence, and our very lives. *Blessed is the man that walketh not in the counsel of the ungodly.* (Psalm 1:1)
Outline:

> Verses 1-4 – Ahaziah, who reigned in Judah after his father's death, continued in the wickedness of his father because he followed the counsel of his father's advisers and that of his mother who was from Israel's idolatrous royal family.
>
> Verses 5-9 – When Ahaziah joined with the Israelites to fight against Syria, the Lord used Jehu to bring judgment and death to him and his princes.
>
> Verses 10-12 – Ahaziah's mother, Athaliah of the royal family in Israel, took the throne in Judah after her son's death. Her first act was to kill her own grandchildren to secure her place by removing any possible contenders for the throne; however, her diabolic scheme was spoiled when Joash was secretly hidden away.

Prayer Focus: Lord, make me sensitive enough to Your Spirit that I will discern when my advisers are not counseling me according to Your heart and mind. Amen.
Notes:

Spiritual Journal:

Week: Forty-one
Day: Tuesday
Book: II Chronicles
Chapter: Twenty-three
Memory Verse: Twenty-one
Principle: We can experience true peace only when we abandon the evil that dictated our lives – whether on the individual internal basis or the external national level.
Outline:

Verses 1-11 – After hiding Joash for seven years, Jehoiada the priest developed a plan to crown him king at the time of the changing of the guard in the Temple on the Sabbath. This would be the most inconspicuous time to maneuver so many of the forces without notice since all the people would be gathered in the Temple compound. At exactly the right moment, the young prince was presented to the people and proclaimed to be king.

Verses 12-15 – When Athaliah heard what was going on, she ran toward the crowd declaring that they were committing treason; however, Jehoiada's forces captured and executed her.

Verses 16-20 – Upon the establishment of a covenant by Jehoiada that the nation would be dedicated to God, the people rushed to the pagan Temple to destroy the building and execute its priest. Once the Temple to Baal was razed, Jehoiada established overseers to ensure that the Temple of God was properly reverenced.

Verse 21 – Upon the removal of the evil dictator, the people rejoiced and the nation of Israel experienced peace.

Prayer Focus: Lord, may I always have the wisdom to recognize evil – whether working inside myself or as an outside force trying to rule me – and the boldness and the spiritual authority to attack and overcome it. Amen.

Notes:

Spiritual Journal:

Week: Forty-one
Day: Wednesday
Book: II Chronicles
Chapter: Twenty-four
Memory Verse: Seventeen
Principle: How we finish the race – not how we begin it – is what counts.
Outline:

> Verses 1-14 – Because he had determined to repair the Temple that had been desecrated by the sons of Athaliah, Joash instructed the priests and Levites to collect funds from the citizenry to cover the costs of the project. When they failed to follow through on his directive, Joash implemented a system of collection in which the people were to bring their offerings into the Temple and place them into a collection box. This new approach was very successful and the renovation project was readily financed and completed.

> Verses 15-22 – After the death of Jehoiada at 130 years of age, the leaders of Judah approached Joash requesting permission to execute Zechariah, the son of Jehoiada, because he had spoken out boldly against their idolatry. Unfortunately, the king joined in with their sinfulness in permitting the execution of this godly messenger.

> Verses 23-27 – As judgment, God allowed a small army of Syrian invaders to claim a great victory against the kingdom of Judah. When they withdrew, the Syrians left behind the severely wounded King Joash who was soon assassinated by his own servants. Even though he had started out as a great leader, his reign ended in such disrepute that he was not granted burial in the royal cemetery.

Prayer Focus: Lord, may I stand firm to the very end, as Your very words instruct that it is only those who endure until the end who shall be saved. (Matthew 24:13) Amen.

Notes:

Spiritual Journal:

Week: Forty-one
Day: Thursday
Book: II Chronicles
Chapter: Twenty-five
Memory Verse: Two
Principle: Our inward attitude is more significant than our outward actions.
Outline:

> Verses 1-4 – When Amaziah became king, he executed the men who had assassinated his father. Although he followed the biblical commandment that he should not also execute their children, his heart attitude must have been that he should have killed them as well.

> Verses 5-13 – When Amaziah went to war against Edom, he hired one hundred thousand Israelite mercenaries to assist him. After being warned by a prophet that the Lord was not with the Israelites, he paid the hired forces their full wage and dismissed them. He then waged a very successful attack against the enemy forces; however, he suffered losses at the hands of the hired army who attacked the border cities in retaliation for the dismissal which they considered to be an insult.

> Verses 14-16 – When Amaziah brought the gods of the Edomites back to Judah and began to worship them, the prophet challenged him that there was no logic in worshiping gods which he himself had demonstrated to be powerless to protect their devotees. When the king threatened to kill the prophet for his words, the prophet left with one final word that God would destroy the king.

> Verses 17-24 – Inspired by the victory over the Edomites and angered by the raids of the mercenaries, Amaziah challenged Israel to battle. Joash replied with a parabolic message warning him not to be lifted up with false security because of the conquest in Edom. Ignoring the warning, Amaziah entered into the conflict, which cost him severely in the destruction of the city, the capture of the national treasury, and the taking of many hostages.

> Verses 25-28 – When Amaziah became aware that there was a conspiracy afoot against him, he tried to escape to Lachish; however, he was pursued, captured, and executed.

Prayer Focus: Lord, grant me true integrity that I may always act because I know in my heart that my actions are in accordance with Your will, not simply in order to comply with the social norm. Amen.
Notes & Spiritual Journal:

Week: Forty-one
Day: Friday
Book: II Chronicles
Chapter: Twenty-six
Memory Verse: Five
Principle: Although destiny is truly in the hand of God, we determine our course by whether we seek God or ignore His directions.
Outline:
Verses 1-5 – Uzziah (also known as Azariah) succeeded his father. Uzziah's fifty-two year reign was marked with great prosperity as long as he sought God.

Verses 6-15 – Uzziah's reign was marked with prosperity in every area: conquest of his enemies, building projects, commercial and agricultural enterprise, international trade, military power, and creative inventions.

Verses 16-23 – Having been such a success in so many areas, the king assumed that he could take the priestly privilege of going into the Temple to burn incense before the altar of God. When the priests challenged his action, the king resisted angrily rather than accepting correction. He was immediately struck with leprosy, which resulted in his having to spend the remaining years of his life in isolation.

Prayer Focus: Lord, help me to always be sensitive to Your Spirit so that I will never assume that I can act outside Your direction and still live inside Your provision. Amen.

Notes:

Spiritual Journal:

Week: Forty-two
Day: Monday
Book: II Chronicles
Chapter: Twenty-seven
Memory Verse: Two
Principle: Godly leadership may not necessarily guarantee righteousness in the people.
Outline:

> Verses 1-9 – Jotham, who reigned after his father's death, was a godly ruler. His sixteen-year rule was marked with prosperity; however, the people did not experience a spiritual renewal during his time of leadership.

Prayer Focus: Lord, may my life not only please You, but let it also lead others to You. Amen.

Notes:

Spiritual Journal:

Week: Forty-two

Day: Tuesday

Book: II Chronicles

Chapter: Twenty-seven

Memory Verse: Twenty-two

Principle: Although non-Christians sometimes come to the Lord as a result of trouble in their lives, the Bible teaches that it is the goodness of God which leads men to repentance.(Romans 2:4)

Outline:

Verses 1-4 – When Ahaz became king in Judah, he followed after the pagan ways of the Canaanites, including child sacrifice.

Verses 5-8 – Because of this paganism, the Lord delivered Judah to the Syrians and the Israelites, at whose hands they suffered great losses.

Verses 9-15 – When a prophet of God admonished the Israelites that they should not take the captives of Judah as slaves, they obediently released them and gave them the necessary supplies for the return journey to their homes.

Verses 16-21 – Because Ahaz had led his nation into sin and immorality, the Lord allowed the Philistines and Edomites to invade Judah. Facing their attacks, Ahaz hired the Assyrians to help him; however, Tiglath-Pileser double-crossed him by taking the spoil but refusing to assist.

Verses 22-25 – Rather than running to God in his time of trouble, Ahaz ran further from Him and began to sacrifice to the gods of the Syrians, thinking that he should win favor with these deities because their help must have been the reason that the Syrians had been successful in their conflict against Judah.

Verses 26-27 – Although Ahaz was buried in Jerusalem, he was not granted a tomb among the kings of Judah.

Prayer Focus: Lord, help me always to realize that You are the source of my solutions, not my problems, and that I must always run to You rather than away from You in my times of difficulty. Amen.

Notes:

Spiritual Journal:

Week: Forty-two
Day: Wednesday
Book: II Chronicles
Chapter: Twenty-nine
Memory Verse: Thirty-one
Principle: Sanctifying and consecrating ourselves unto the Lord qualifies us to then enter boldly into His presence. (Hebrews 4:15-16)
Outline:

> Verses 1-19 – Immediately upon his ascent to the throne, Hezekiah purposed to purge the Temple and re-establish a covenant with God in atonement for the wickedness of his predecessors. Having incorporated the assistance of the Levites and the priesthood, he was able to readily accomplish the cleansing of the Temple.
>
> Verses 20-36 – Through a blood sacrifice accompanied with praise and worship, the priests consecrated the Temple and the people to God. The overwhelming response required that more assistants be recruited to help handle the sacrifices; the promptness with which the people responded demonstrated that it was indeed God's plan that the nation be rededicated to Him.

Prayer Focus: Lord, help me to be quick to yield to You in repentance and service. Amen.
Notes:

Spiritual Journal:

Week: Forty-two
Day: Thursday
Book: II Chronicles
Chapter: Thirty
Memory Verse: Nineteen
Principle: Although God does require us to adhere to His commandments, He is more in tune with our heart attitude than with our physical performance.
Outline:

Verses 1-12 – When Hezekiah proposed a special celebration of the Passover a month late because the priesthood had not been properly prepared to execute their functions at the appointed time of the Passover during the first month, his proposal was met by disdain from some and hearty acceptance by others.

Verses 13-27 – Although some of the participants were not ceremonially prepared for the sacred celebration, the Lord honored their heart's desire and accepted their worship. The jubilant celebration continued for two full weeks as the participants sacrificed animals by the thousands unto the Lord.

Prayer Focus: Lord, knowing that You look on my heart, I ask that You help me to keep my heart right before You. Also knowing that men look on the outward appearance, I desire that You also assist me in living my daily life in accordance with all Your precepts. I trust You to work in me both to will and to do Your good pleasure. (Philippians 2:13) Amen.

Notes:

Spiritual Journal:

Week: Forty-two
Day: Friday
Book: II Chronicles
Chapter: Thirty-one
Memory Verse: Twenty-one
Principle: Whatsoever ye do, do it heartily, as to the Lord. (Colossians 2:23)
Outline:

> Verses 1-19 – Once the great covenant renewal celebration and the cleansing of the land was completed, the priests and Levites returned to their homes. When Hezekiah implemented a collection to support them, the people responded in a way that was more than sufficient for the need.

> Verses 20-21 – Hezekiah's reign was marked with prosperity resulting from his diligent obedience to the Lord's commandments and righteousness.

Prayer Focus: Lord, may my life be characterized by success stemming from a radical obedience to Your commandments and sincere love for You. Amen.

Notes:

Spiritual Journal:

Week: Forty-three
Day: Monday
Book: II Chronicles
Chapter: Thirty-two
Memory Verse: Twenty
Principle: When God's people pray, things change.
Outline:

> Verses 1-8 – Facing an invasion by the Syrians, Hezekiah responded by cutting off the water supply that the enemy forces would need to sustain themselves during the campaign, by enhancing the city's defense and armaments, and by encouraging the people to be courageous and full of faith.

> Verses 9-19 – Sennacherib tried to weaken the people's morale and convince them to surrender by challenging their faith in Hezekiah and the God he had taught them to trust.

> Verses 20-22 – Because of the earnest intercession of the king and the prophet, the Lord delivered Jerusalem, decimating the Syrian army and sending Sennacherib home in humiliation.

> Verses 23-31 – Because of the great victory, followed by a miraculous healing, and his great wealth and accomplishments (which included the construction of an advanced water system for the city of Jerusalem), the king experienced a period of pride, which required his repentance and restoration.

> Verses 32-33 – He died as a man of honor and respect among his people.

Prayer Focus: Lord, when You look for a man to stand in the gap as an intercessor, may You find me ready to help make up the hedge. (Ezekiel 22:30) Amen.

Notes:

Spiritual Journal:

Week: Forty-three
Day: Tuesday
Book: II Chronicles
Chapter: Thirty-three
Memory Verse: Ten
Principle: *Trust in the LORD with all thine heart; and lean not unto thine own understanding. In all thy ways acknowledge him, and he shall direct thy paths. Be not wise in thine own eyes: fear the LORD, and depart from evil.* (Proverbs 3:5-7)
Outline:

> Verses 1-9 – Manasseh's early years were marked with gross idolatry and blatant rebellion against God and righteousness.
>
> Verses 10-20 – As a result of his determined resistance to the warnings of the Lord, Manasseh was delivered into Assyrian captivity where he humbled himself before the Lord and repented. He was then released and returned to Jerusalem where he lived out his life and fostered reform and reconstruction.
>
> Verses 21-25 – Amon's two-year reign, which was characterized by a return to pagan idolatry, ended in a conspiracy and his assassination.

Prayer Focus: Lord, may I never refuse to hear when You speak to me. Amen.
Notes:

Spiritual Journal:

Week: Forty-three
Day: Wednesday
Book: II Chronicles
Chapter: Thirty-four
Memory Verse: Thirty-one
Principle: Men in positions of authority need to make public declarations of their faith and to lead their constituents into godliness.
Outline:
>Verses 1-7 – Although Josiah was only an eight-year-old boy when he became king, his reign was characterized by strong and godly leadership that brought reform to his people.
>
>Verses 8-28 – When his renovation efforts in the Temple uncovered the forgotten Book of the Law, the king was earnestly concerned because his people had been in such serious violation of the recorded statutes of God. When the prophetess Hulda was consulted, she affirmed that the nation would be judged for its gross iniquities but that Josiah would be spared because of his repentant and humble heart.
>
>Verses 29-33 – Josiah personally led the nation in a covenant renewal and reform.

Prayer Focus: Lord, grant me a sphere of influence where I can stand for You. Give me the courage to take a public stand for righteousness and godliness. Amen.

Notes:

Spiritual Journal:

Week: Forty-three
Day: Thursday
Book: II Chronicles
Chapter: Thirty-five
Memory Verse: Twenty-two
Principle: It is vitally important to always listen when God is speaking because a lifetime of good and godly deeds can be negated by one simple action outside the will of God.
Outline:
Verses 1-19 – Josiah elected to mark the Passover with a spectacular celebration, including the restoration of the order of the priests and the Levites and a gala display of worship and sacrifice.
Verses 20-26 – Josiah's remarkable life came to a tragic end because he involved himself in needless conflict after deliberately resisting the voice of God warning him not to involve himself in the matter.
Prayer Focus: Lord, may Paul's advice in I Corinthians 9:27 ever be a focus in my life: *I keep under my body, and bring it into subjection: lest that by any means, when I have preached to others, I myself should be a castaway.* Amen.
Notes:

Spiritual Journal:

Week: Forty-three
Day: Friday
Book: II Chronicles
Chapter: Thirty-six
Memory Verse: Fifteen
Principle: In the best of times and in the worst of times, God is always speaking to His people; it is whether they hear His voice and heed His instructions that determines the future.
Outline:

> Verses 1-14 – Jerusalem's last years before the Babylonian captivity were marked by a series of wicked and weak kings who were dominated by foreign powers.
>
> Verses 15-20 – The people's refusal to heed the prophet's warnings precipitated God's judgment – including the destruction of the city, the confiscation of the treasury, the razing of the Temple, the captivity of the people, and the slaughter of the armed forces.
>
> Verses 21-23 – According to God's faithfulness, He moved King Cyrus to restore His people once their determined punishment had been meted out to them.

Prayer Focus: Lord, thank you for Your promise in Hebrews 13:5 that You will never leave us nor forsake us. Help me to be aware that You are constantly working toward my restoration even if You have to correct and judge me for refusing to hear and heed Your voice. Amen.

Notes:

Spiritual Journal:

Week: Forty-four

Day: Monday

Book: Ezra

Chapter: One

Memory Verse: One

Principle: In order to fulfill His Word and His will, God will use any and every person necessary – saint or sinner, great or small, young or old.

Outline:

> Verses 1-4 – When King Cyrus of Persia declared that the Jewish people were to return to Jerusalem to rebuild the Temple and nation, he fulfilled the prophecy of Jeremiah 25:12 that the nation of Israel would be restored after seventy years of captivity.

> Verses 5-6 – The leaders of Judah and Benjamin were aroused to make the return, and others who were not inclined to return gave them support.

> Verses 7-11 – King Cyrus returned all the treasures that had been confiscated from the Temple.

Prayer Focus: Lord, help me to always expect You to be at work in the world around me and to see Your hand at work – even in unexpected places through unexpected people in unexpected ways. Amen.

Notes:

Spiritual Journal:

Week: Forty-four

Day: Tuesday

Book: Ezra

Chapter: Two

Memory Verse: One

Principle: God is a restorer. It is His plan and purpose to bring us back to the place from which we have fallen and to bring back to us the possessions which have been taken from us.

Outline:

Verses 1-61 – An extensive listing of those who returned from captivity shows the all-inclusive nature of God's plan of restoration.

Verses 62-63 – Provision was made for those whose authenticity was questionable.

Verses 64-67 – A full tally of the people, their servants, and livestock is given.

Verses 68-70 – According to their ability, the returnees gave generously for the reconstruction of the Temple.

Prayer Focus: Lord, my prayer today can be taken from the words of an old gospel song, "Oh, Lord, I want to be in that number when the roll is called up yonder." Amen.

Notes:

Spiritual Journal:

Week: Forty-four
Day: Wednesday
Book: Ezra
Chapter: Three
Memory Verse: Eleven
Principle: God's goodness and mercy are demonstrated in the redemption and restoration of His people.
Outline:
> Verses 1-5 – The people began to observe the appointed sacrifices and celebrate the scheduled holidays even before the Temple construction began.
>
> Verses 6-7 – Procurement of the needed construction materials was arranged.
>
> Verses 8-11 – With great pomp, ceremony, and jubilant praise to the Lord, they laid the foundation stones.
>
> Verses 12-13 – The jubilant celebration was mixed with an emotional lament from those who remembered the original Temple that had been destroyed.

Prayer Focus: Lord, may I celebrate each day as I recognize that Your goodness and mercy are demonstrated daily in my life as You are actively at work redeeming, restoring, and rebuilding. Amen.

Notes:

Spiritual Journal:

Week: Forty-four
Day: Thursday
Book: Ezra
Chapter: Four
Memory Verse: Four
Principle: When we start to do something constructive for the Lord, there will invariably
     be someone or something which will try to stop us or at least impede our progress.
Outline:
     Verses 1-2 – The adversaries first posed as supporters and asked to help.
     Verses 3-5 – When they were not allowed to assist, they began a campaign to
        hinder progress on the reconstruction of the Temple.
     Verses 6-16 – As a last resort, they contacted King Artaxerxes with a petition to
        stop the work, based on the accusation that the Jews would rebel from his
        rule once they had a strong city erected.
     Verses 17-22 – Having read the letter and reviewed the history of Jerusalem, King
        Artaxerxes felt that having a strong city could pose a potential threat and
        ordered that the work should be discontinued.
     Verses 23-24 – The leaders of Jerusalem complied with the king's command and
        ceased the reconstruction project.
Prayer Focus: Lord, grant me discernment to recognize those who would oppose Your
     will in my life – even if they pose as my friends. Grant me spiritual tenacity
     enough to resist all attempts to stop me from fulfilling Your will – even when the
     hindrance comes from high places and in a seemingly official form. Amen.
Notes:

Spiritual Journal:

Week: Forty-four

Day: Friday

Book: Ezra

Chapter: Five

Memory Verse: Five

Principle: The favor of God overpowers every physical or demonic force which tries to hinder His servants.

Outline:

> Verses 1-2 – In response to prophetic command, the elders of Jerusalem and Judah returned to the task of restoring the Temple.
>
> Verses 3-5 – The regional government officials tried to stop the work; but they were unable to overpower the Jewish leaders because the favor of God was upon them and their work.
>
> Verses 6-17 – The regional governor sent a letter to King Darius recounting the charges he was pressing against the Jewish leaders along with their claim that their work was mandated and supported by King Cyrus. He then requested that an inquiry be made to determine if the Jews' claim could be substantiated.

Prayer Focus: Lord, I ask for Your favor to overshadow my daily life. Amen.

Notes:

Spiritual Journal:

Week: Forty-five
Day: Monday
Book: Ezra
Chapter: Six
Memory Verse: Fourteen
Principle: God has a way of turning what was meant for evil against His children to their benefit. (Genesis 50:20)
Outline:

> Verses 1-12 – When Darius searched his archives, he discovered Cyrus' original decree concerning the rebuilding of the Temple and commanded that those who had set out to stop the work should not only allow it to be completed but should also financially support the expensive undertaking.
>
> Verses 13-14 – Under divine favor of God and with human support, the work progressed rapidly.
>
> Verses 15-18 – The dedication of the rebuilt Temple was a joyous event marked with great pomp and ceremony and abundant sacrifices.
>
> Verses 19-22 – The celebration of the Passover was an especially joyful event as the people rejoiced in how God had turned the heart of the king to bless them rather than to hinder them.

Prayer Focus: Lord, today thank you for Your promises:

> those who oppose me will be condemned (Isaiah 54:17),
>
> those who try to trap me will be snared by their own devices (Ecclesiastes 10:8),
>
> You will make my enemies to be at peace with me (Psalm 16:7), and
>
> I can live in favor not only with God but also with men (Luke 2:52). Amen.

Notes:

Spiritual Journal:

Week: Forty-five

Day: Tuesday

Book: Ezra

Chapter: Seven

Memory Verse: Twenty-seven

Principle: God can use anyone – even unbelievers – to express His favor toward His children.

Outline:

Verses 1-10 – Accompanied by priests, Levites, and other officials, the skilled scribe Ezra made the four-month journey from Babylon to Jerusalem to instruct the people in the statutes of the Lord.

Verses 11-26 – He brought with him a letter from King Artaxerxes detailing his permission for the Temple to be rebuilt, his provision for the supplies to be given, and his prohibition for anyone to hinder the work.

Verses 27-28 – Encouraged by the divine favor that was extended to him through the provision of the earthly king, Ezra gathered the leading men of Israel to motivate them.

Prayer Focus: Lord, thank you for Your favor and for the variety of ways You use to convey it to me. Amen.

Notes:

Spiritual Journal:

Week: Forty-five

Day: Wednesday

Book: Ezra

Chapter: Eight

Memory Verse: Twenty-two

Principle: We should have so much confidence in the Lord's provision for us that we would be ashamed to ask for human intervention.

Outline:

Verses 1-20 – When Ezra collected the people of Israel, he realized that the family of Levi was not represented, so he recruited men from that tribe to join the others who stood with him.

Verses 21-23 – Rather than request physical protection from the human king, Ezra called the people to fast and pray for divine protection as they traveled to Jerusalem.

Verses 24-30 – The treasures were dispersed among the travelers for safekeeping.

Verses 31-36 – Upon safely reaching Jerusalem, they delivered the treasures to the Temple, made sacrifices unto the Lord, and delivered the king's edict to the regional rulers.

Prayer Focus: Lord, may my life follow the pattern of the psalmist who said that he would continually boast in the Lord. (Psalm 34:2) Amen.

Notes:

Spiritual Journal:

Week: Forty-five
Day: Thursday
Book: Ezra
Chapter: Nine
Memory Verse: Thirteen
Principle: God is a restorer. Even in His judgments against our sinfulness, He extends mercy and restoration to the sinner who seeks His pardon.
Outline:
Verses 1-4 – When Ezra learned that the people of Jerusalem – including the religious and civil leaders – had intermarried with the pagan people of the region, he was astonished and spent the whole day in mourning.

Verses 5-15 – His intercession for the situation was based on the fact that God had granted favor to the people even when they were in exile due to their transgressions. Now, he repented for the unthinkable deeds of the people who would so blatantly violate the commandments of God after having experienced His great mercy. Confessing that the people were not even worthy to stand before Him, much less ask for His mercy, Ezra appealed to the righteousness of God.

Prayer Focus: Lord, grant me the humility of heart it takes to recognize Your hand of mercy upon my life and to respond to that mercy with righteousness rather than continued disobedience. Amen.
Notes:

Spiritual Journal:

Week: Forty-five
Day: Friday
Book: Ezra
Chapter: Ten
Memory Verse: Four
Principle: We must learn to know when it is our time to take responsibility and act.
Outline:

> Verses 1-4 – As Ezra fasted and prayed, the men of Israel gathered around him and encouraged him to take action concerning the intermarriage of the people with their pagan neighbors.
>
> Verses 5-8 – Ezra made a proclamation that everyone should appear before him under penalty of loss of property and banishment for anyone who failed to comply.
>
> Verses 9-15 – All the men gathered, even in a heavy rain, to hear Ezra's message concerning the guilt of their pagan relationships and his proposal for them to dissolve these marriages. Because of the magnitude of the task and the very bad weather, it was decided to deal with the cases by locality – a process which took three months to complete. In spite of the immensity of this undertaking, only four people resisted.
>
> Verses 16-17 – Questioning was carried out among all those who had pagan wives.
>
> Verses 18-44 – Record is given of those who put away their pagan wives and the children which had been born to them.

Prayer Focus: Lord, grant me wisdom to know when I must take responsibility – and courage to act at those times. Amen.
Notes:

Spiritual Journal:

Week: Forty-six
Day: Monday
Book: Nehemiah
Chapter: One
Memory Verse: Four
Principle: A true man of God is moved to prayer and action by the needs of others.
Outline:

Verses 1-3 – When Nehemiah heard the condition of his brethren and the city of Jerusalem, he was motivated to intercede and act on their behalf.

Verses 4-11 – Because Nehemiah's prayer contains all the elements of a great prayer, it can become a model for intercession:

a) He began by magnifying the Lord through recognizing His authority, sovereignty, and merciful compassion.

b) He humbled himself before the Lord by calling himself a servant.

c) He expressed determination when he said that he would pray day and night.

d) He confessed his own sin and the sin of the people.

e) He reviewed the promises and covenants of the Lord concerning the present situation.

f) When he mentioned that God had already restored the people to the land, he was acknowledging how God was already at work.

g) He expressed his readiness to be used as part of the answer when he mentioned his position as the cupbearer to the king, whose heart he was asking the Lord to touch.

Prayer Focus: Lord, make me an intercessor – both in prayer and in action. Amen.
Notes:

Spiritual Journal:

Week: Forty-six
Day: Tuesday
Book: Nehemiah
Chapter: Two
Memory Verse: Three
Principle: It is the Christian's responsibility to bear the burdens of others. *Bear ye one another's burdens, and so fulfill the law of Christ.* (Galatians 6:2) *Rejoice with them that do rejoice, and weep with them that weep.* (Romans 12:15)
Outline:

> Verses 1-3 – When the king noticed sadness on Nehemiah's face, he inquired what his problem was. After a quick prayer for divinely guided words, Nehemiah answered that he lamented the fact that his homeland lay in ruins.

> Verses 4-8 – The king responded by granting Nehemiah permission to go to Jerusalem to rebuild the walls. He also granted Nehemiah's further request for letters to the governors of the region authorizing him to do the work and requiring them to furnish him with the necessary supplies.

> Verses 9-10 – The local rulers were very displeased with Nehemiah's arrival and his intent to restore the city.

> Verses 11-16 – Under cloak of night, Nehemiah surveyed the condition of the city's walls.

> Verses 17-20 – When Nehemiah challenged the people to arise to repair the breaches in the walls, the regional governors mocked his proposal and called it rebellion against the king. Nehemiah's response was that it was a God-ordained project and that He would cause it to prosper.

Prayer Focus: Lord, my prayer today is patterned after that of a great missionary who daily prayed, "Break my heart with the things that break Yours." Amen.
Notes:

Spiritual Journal:

Week: Forty-six

Day: Wednesday

Book: Nehemiah

Chapter: Three

Memory Verse: One

Principle: As individual members in the Body of Christ, we must all do our own individual part so that, as the corporate Body of Christ, we are able to fulfill the purposes of God in our present world. (Romans 12:4-5, Ephesians 4:16)

Outline:

Verses 1-32 – Each member of the community – whether a religious leader, a political official, a merchant, or a common laborer – took charge of repairing a specific portion of the wall around the city of Jerusalem.

Prayer Focus: Lord, help me to have the humility to always do my part and not be concerned with whether it fits my "job description." Amen.

Notes:

Spiritual Journal:

Week: Forty-six
Day: Thursday
Book: Nehemiah
Chapter: Four
Memory Verse: Seventeen
Principle: Vigilance and industry are twin keys to success, just as having a strong defense and a strong offense are the winning combination for any game.
Outline:

> Verses 1-12 – When the adversaries saw how the workers willingly built the wall and the progress they were making, they plotted to sabotage the work through sudden attacks. Aware of the impending danger, the Jews prayed to God and called upon Nehemiah to help them.

> Verses 13-23 – Nehemiah's plan was to combine the defense and offense by having half the servants stand guard while the other half worked. In addition, the workers were armed so that they could fight as readily as they could build. All the laborers stayed at the construction sight around the clock to protect the work, and each man was in a constant state of readiness, indicated by remaining fully clothed and armed at all times except for bathing.

Prayer Focus: Lord, grant me the supernatural wisdom to see how I must be both a defender and an aggressor in order to establish Your kingdom in this world. Amen.

Notes:

Spiritual Journal:

Week: Forty-six
Day: Friday
Book: Nehemiah
Chapter: Five
Memory Verse: Nine
Principle: Nehemiah's personal actions exemplified the "Golden Rule" in which Jesus taught us that we should do unto others as we would have them do unto us. The demands that he placed upon the community leaders exemplified the requirements of God which the prophet Micah enumerated for us when he said that we should love mercy, do justly, and walk humbly before our God.

Outline:
Verses 1-5 – The local citizenry pleaded for Nehemiah to intervene for them in their desperation, which had led many of them to such extreme poverty that they had sold their children into slavery.

Verses 6-13 – Nehemiah confronted the nobles and rulers concerning their greed and insensitivity to the people. He challenged them over their error in demanding high taxes and imposing usury upon the people. When he accused the rulers and nobles of bringing the people into bondage after God Himself had just delivered them from slavery among the nations, they repented and promised to restore the people. Nehemiah responded with a dramatic illustration depicting the total ruin that God would bring upon anyone who failed to fulfill this pledge.

Verses 14-19 – Nehemiah refused to accept any personal compensation for his twelve years of service in Jerusalem because of his reverence for the Lord and empathy for the common people who bore the burden of the taxes. Although he hosted a large entourage at his table daily, he supplied all the provisions himself rather than accepting public funds.

Prayer Focus: Lord, may I be able to live as John F. Kennedy declared in his famous address when inaugurated as President of the United States, "Ask not what your country can do for you; ask what you can do for your country!" Amen.

Notes:

Spiritual Journal:

Week: Forty-seven
Day: Monday
Book: Nehemiah
Chapter: Six
Memory Verse: Three
Principle: We must be so totally focused on fulfilling the will and purpose of the Lord that we cannot be stirred to the right or left, hindered, or discouraged in our resolve.
Outline:
>Verses 1-4 – Nervous because Nehemiah had been successful in rebuilding the walls of the city, Sanballat and Tobiah schemed to assassinate him after luring him away from the safety of the city. Nehemiah, however, refused their requests by pointing to the important work he was doing and saying that he could not stop to meet with them.

>Verses 5-9 – Their fifth attempt to dissuade Nehemiah from his work involved the psychology of sending an open letter intended to instill fear into the hearts of the people.

>Verses 10-14 – Their next ploy was to hire a double agent to pose as a prophet who would advise Nehemiah to seek refuge in the inner courts of the Temple. Discerning that this message was part of a plot to instill fear and to discredit his reputation, Nehemiah responded that he was too much of a man of faith to hide from any danger – whether real or imagined.

>Verses 15-16 – To the dismay and chagrin of his opponents, Nehemiah completed the task of repairing the walls of the city in only fifty-two days.

>Verses 17-19 – Because he had family ties with leaders in Jerusalem, Tobiah was able to continue to get communications and propaganda into the city.

Prayer Focus: Lord, help me to always be so focused on completing Your will that nothing can turn me from it. Amen.
Notes:

Spiritual Journal:

Week: Forty-seven

Day: Tuesday

Book: Nehemiah

Chapter: Seven

Memory Verse: Two

Principle: The person who is faithful over a few things will be made ruler over many. (Matthew 25:23)

Outline:

> Verses 1-3 – When the rebuilding of the wall was completed, Nehemiah placed his brother, who had proven himself through his faithfulness and godly devotion, in charge of regulating the city gates.

> Verses 4-73 – When Nehemiah next turned his attention to a census of the people, he based his registration upon the records that had been made at the time of the first return from the captivity.

Prayer Focus: Lord, my desire is to be a faithful steward and a God-fearing servant – not because I desire to be promoted to being a ruler – simply because I want to have a character which is pleasing to You. Amen.

Notes:

Spiritual Journal:

Week: Forty-seven
Day: Wednesday
Book: Nehemiah
Chapter: Eight
Memory Verse: Ten
Principle: Understanding and following the Law of God is not grievous; rather, it is a source of joy and strength.
Outline:
Verses 1-12 – Ezra and Nehemiah collected the people of Israel for a mass assembly in which they read and interpreted the Law to them. When the people responded sorrowfully because of their having broken the commandments of the Law, Ezra and Nehemiah reassured them that this was an occasion to rejoice rather than mourn, because they were being given a chance to understand the requirements of God and to begin to obey them.
Verses 13-18 – When they read of the requirements for observing the Feast of Tabernacles, the people immediately complied and spent seven days living in booths and listening to the reading of the Law.
Prayer Focus: Lord, may I always be ready to hear and obey Your statutes. Amen.
Notes:

Spiritual Journal:

Week: Forty-seven

Day: Thursday

Book: Nehemiah

Chapter: Nine

Memory Verse: Thirty-one

Principle: God's mercy (His undeserved favor) elicits our humble gratitude and repentant obedience.

Outline:

> Verses 1-5 – The people of God separated themselves from the gentiles and observed a special time of intensive and extensive soul-searching and penance.
>
> Verses 6-37 – They recited the history of the mercy God had shown to them even in the face of their rebellious defiance of His commandments.
>
> Verse 38 – Their conclusion was to renew their covenant relationship with the Lord.

Prayer Focus: Lord, may I always respond to Your mercy toward me with unquestioning obedience and unwavering humility. Amen.

Notes:

Spiritual Journal:

Week: Forty-seven
Day: Friday
Book: Nehemiah
Chapter: Ten
Memory Verse: Twenty-nine
Principle: Covenanting with God has both a positive and negative side: there is tremendous blessing in store for those who obey the ordinances of the covenant, but a curse for those who are aware of the requirements of the covenant and fail to observe them.
Outline:

> Verses 1-27 – A listing is given of those who pledged themselves in covenant relationship to God.
>
> Verses 28-39 – The people committed themselves to observing the prohibitions against intermarriage with foreigners, buying and selling on the Sabbath, planting during the sabbatical year, and extracting usury from fellow Israelites. They also committed themselves to tithing, giving offerings, and observing the special religious holidays.

Prayer Focus: Lord, help me to have the courage to give myself wholly to You, aware of the consequences as well as the advantages. Amen.
Notes:

Spiritual Journal:

Week: Forty-eight
Day: Monday
Book: Nehemiah
Chapter: Eleven
Memory Verse: Two
Principle: Living with God, in His presence and by His principles, is a free choice that we
    should make willingly.
Outline:
    Verses 1-3 – While the leadership was given automatic residence in Jerusalem,
        the laymen who were to live in the city were chosen by lot.
    Verses 4-24 – A register of those who were to dwell in the city is given.
    Verses 25-36 – Those who were to inhabit the outlying region are enumerated.
Prayer Focus: Lord, may I never hesitate to choose to live with and for You. Amen.
Notes:

Spiritual Journal:

Week: Forty-eight
Day: Tuesday
Book: Nehemiah
Chapter: Twelve
Memory Verse: Forty-three
Principle: Our praise to the Lord should be unashamedly expressive.
Outline:

> Verses 1-26 – A listing is given of the priests and spiritual leaders who were summoned to participate in the dedication ceremony of the rebuilt walls.
>
> Verses 27-43 – Jubilant praise along with majestic pomp and ceremony characterized the dedication of the city wall.
>
> Verses 44-47 – Praise, generosity, and sanctification summarized the functions of those who devoted themselves to the Lord and His service.

Prayer Focus: Lord, just as did the Levites of old, may I also live a life characterized by praise, generosity, and sanctification. Amen.

Notes:

Spiritual Journal:

Week: Forty-eight
Day: Wednesday
Book: Nehemiah
Chapter: Thirteen
Memory Verse: Fourteen
Principle: As Christians, we must live lives which are marked with good works worthy of notice and commendation.
Outline:

> Verses 1-3 – Based on Balaam's attempt to curse Israel, the Ammonites and Moabites were separated from the people of Israel and excluded from the Temple.
>
> Verses 4-9 – When Nehemiah learned that Eliashib the priest (who had a relationship with the enemy through marriage) had provided quarters for Tobiah in the Temple, he had the intruder removed and the chambers cleaned and restored to their original purpose.
>
> Verses 10-13 – When he saw that the Temple workers had returned to secular employment because they were not receiving payment for their sacred duties, Nehemiah insisted that the offerings and distributions be re-instituted.
>
> Verse 14 – Nehemiah breathed a prayer that his good works not go unnoticed.
>
> Verses 15-22 – In response to having seen people working and doing business on the Sabbath, Nehemiah had the gates to the city locked on the holy day in order to keep out all those who would attempt to pursue commerce.
>
> Verses 23-28 – Nehemiah resorted to personally inflict corporal punishment on those who had intermarried with the local people.
>
> Verses 29-31 – Nehemiah requests God's blessings as he summarizes his reform.

Prayer Focus: Lord, may my life be filled with good deeds worthy of recognition and remembrance. Amen.
Notes:

Spiritual Journal:

Week: Forty-eight
Day: Thursday
Book: Esther
Chapter: One
Memory Verse: Four
Principle: There is no place for flamboyant pretense in the kingdom of God; all recognition and attention should be drawn and directed to God, not ourselves and our human accomplishments or possessions.
Outline:
Verses 1-9 – King Ahasuerus of Persia held a six-month-long national celebration climaxed by a seven-day royal feast.
Verses 10-12 – As a closing event to the feast, he commanded Queen Vashti to make an appearance at the feast; however, she refused his order.
Verses 13-22 – Upon the advice of his counselors, the king had Vashti stripped of all her royal position and privilege.
Prayer Focus: Lord, help me guard myself against pride, arrogance, boasting, and ostentation. Amen.
Notes:

Spiritual Journal:

Week: Forty-eight
Day: Friday
Book: Esther
Chapter: Two
Memory Verse: Fifteen
Principle: A godly woman has beauty which is not *outward adorning of plaiting the hair, of wearing of gold, or of putting on of apparel, but...the hidden man of the heart ...which is not corruptible, even the ornament of a meek and quiet spirit, which is in the sight of God of great price.* (I Peter 3:3-4)
Outline:
> Verses 1-4 – An elaborate search for a beautiful maiden to replace Queen Vashti involved an empire-wide beauty contest.
>
> Verses 5-13 – Esther, an orphaned Jewish girl who had been raised by her cousin Mordecai, was selected as one of the candidates for the king's approval.
>
> Verses 14-18 – The king loved her and selected her as his new queen.
>
> Verses 19-20 – Because of his cousin's position as the new queen, Mordecai was privileged to sit in the king's gate where much of the political debate was held and many of the national decisions were made.
>
> Verses 21-23 – In the king's gate, Mordecai learned of a plot against the king. By communicating his inside information to Esther, he was able to save the king's life.

Prayer Focus: Lord, regardless of whether I am male or female, I pray that the qualities of the inner man outshine the frailty of my outer personality. Amen.
Notes:

Spiritual Journal:

Week: Forty-nine
Day: Monday
Book: Esther
Chapter: Three
Memory Verse: Eight
Principle: As Christians, we are citizens of a different kingdom (Philippians 3:20), and we cannot live like others who are merely earthly citizens. We must live within the laws and customs of the land as much as is possible, but we must always remain true to the ordinances of our true homeland if there is a conflict between them, remembering that we live in the present world as mere aliens. (1 Peter 2:11)
Outline:
Verses 1-5 – When Haman was elevated to one of the highest positions in the kingdom, he was extremely upset that Mordecai – because of his religious convictions – refused to show him homage.
Verses 6-15 – Haman's anger was so great that he devised a plan in which he would not only take vengeance upon Mordecai but would also destroy all the Jews who shared Mordecai's religion. He convinced the king to sign a decree that a certain day be set aside on which the Jews would be slaughtered and to set a budget for carrying out this massacre. Official mandates were sent throughout the empire requiring that each district participate in the planned melee.
Prayer Focus: Lord, grant me conviction to recognize when the laws and customs of man are in conflict with the statutes of God and the courage to stand for You in the face of all human and demonic opposition. Amen.
Notes:

Spiritual Journal:

Week: Forty-nine
Day: Tuesday
Book: Esther
Chapter: Four
Memory Verse: Fourteen
Principle: We must recognize that God has orchestrated our lives and placed us strategically where we are to impact the world around us for His kingdom.
Outline:

> Verses 1-3 – Mordecai, along with Jews throughout the kingdom, responded to the decree with mourning and the symbolic act of dressing in sackcloth.
>
> Verses 4-9 – When Esther learned of Mordecai's actions, she sent him new clothes, but he refused to accept them. His response to her was that she should go to the king and make supplication on behalf of her people.
>
> Verses 10-14 – Esther responded that, under penalty of death, she could not approach the king unless he beckoned her. Mordecai advised her that her life was in danger already because she would be included in the coming extermination. He challenged her to consider that the whole purpose she had been given a place of status in the kingdom was to position her to act on behalf of God's people.
>
> Verses 15-17 – Esther accepted her cousin's challenge but requested that all the Jews fast and intercede for three days on her behalf before she approached the monarch.

Prayer Focus: Lord, help me to recognize every advantage You have given me and help me to have the courage and wisdom to use each of my opportunities to establish Your kingdom. Amen.

Notes:

Spiritual Journal:

Week: Forty-nine
Day: Wednesday
Book: Esther
Chapter: Five
Memory Verse: Nine
Principle: Even when everything is going our way in life, we cannot be truly happy if we
      have evil in our hearts.
Outline:
      Verses 1-8 – When Esther presented herself before the king, he approved her and
          offered to grant her request. She responded by inviting the king and
          Haman to a banquet. When the king again inquired concerning her
          request, she requested that he and Haman come to yet another banquet the
          following day.
      Verses 9-13 – Although he was elated by his special privilege of being the private
          guest at a royal banquet, Haman's pride was insulted by Mordecai's
          refusal to show homage to him. Upon reciting all his status, wealth, and
          privilege, Haman concluded that none of it satisfied him as long as
          Mordecai refused to acknowledge him.
      Verse 14 – Haman was put at ease by the suggestion of his wife and friends that
          he request that the king have Mordecai executed.
Prayer Focus: Lord, guard me against pride and selfishness. Amen.
Notes:

Spiritual Journal:

Week: Forty-nine
Day: Thursday
Book: Esther
Chapter: Six
Memory Verse: Thirteen
Principle: Genesis 12:3 promises that God will bless those who bless the Jewish people but curse those who curse them.
Outline:

> Verses 1-3 – On the same night that Haman decided to ask that Mordecai be executed, the king was reminded of how Mordecai had saved his life and decided to do something to honor him for his noble act.
>
> Verses 4-10 – When Haman entered the king's chamber ready to ask for Mordecai's death warrant, the king asked his advice on how to honor someone with whom the king was delighted. Thinking that it was himself whom the king wanted to honor, Haman devised an elaborate display of pageantry for the recipient of the king's favor.
>
> Verses 11-14 – The tables were turned when the king directed Haman to show this great respect to Mordecai. When he told his family and friends about this humiliating experience, they advised him that he was destined for calamity because he was trying to curse God's special people.

Prayer Focus: Lord, may I always remember that Your promises are to the Jew first and also to the Greek (Romans 1:16) and that the blessings I have received are only mine because I have been grafted into the spiritual heritage of Your chosen people (Romans 11:17). Amen.

Notes:

Spiritual Journal:

Week: Forty-nine
Day: Friday
Book: Esther
Chapter: Seven
Memory Verse: Ten
Principle: When we determine evil against others, we become the victims of our own schemes. Proverbs 26:27 puts it this way, *Whoso diggeth a pit shall fall therein.*
Outline:

Verses 1-4 – When the king asked Esther what her petition was, she answered him with a request that she and her people be spared from the planned annihilation.

Verses 5-7 – When he learned that Haman was behind the evil plot, the disturbed king went to the garden to collect his thoughts. While the king was outside the room, Haman begged Esther to spare his life.

Verses 8-10 – Upon his return, the king found Haman grasping for Esther and assumed that he was attempting to assault her. With increased rage, he demanded Haman's arrest and agreed to the suggestion that he be hanged on the same gallows that had been erected for Mordecai's execution.

Prayer Focus: Lord, teach me to always purpose good, not evil, for others so that I will reap blessing from the good seeds I have sown into others' lives. Amen.

Notes:

Spiritual Journal:

Week: Fifty
Day: Monday
Book: Esther
Chapter: Eight
Memory Verse: Seventeen
Principle: When God steps into a desperate situation, He turns the despair into rejoicing.

> *Thou hast turned for me my mourning into dancing: thou hast put off my sackcloth, and girded me with gladness.* (Psalm 30:11) No matter what has been planned against His people, God always has a plan to turn it for the believers' benefit. *But as for you, ye thought evil against me; but God meant it unto good, to bring to pass, as it is this day, to save much people alive.* (Genesis 50:20)

Outline:

> Verses 1-2 – Haman's property and wealth were given to Esther, and his position was given to Mordecai.
>
> Verses 3-8 – When Esther asked the king that he do something to rescue the Jews from annihilation, he gave Esther and Mordecai full authority to make any royal decree they wished concerning the matter.
>
> Verses 9-14 – Because they could not reverse the original decree, they simply added to it that the Jews were to be permitted to defend themselves and to destroy their enemies rather than to be destroyed by them.
>
> Verses 15-17 – The lament of the Jews became jubilance, and many people of the land converted to the Jewish faith.

Prayer Focus: Lord, help me to always believe that You do have a silver lining waiting for me on the other side of the dark clouds which come into my life. Amen.

Notes:

Spiritual Journal:

Week: Fifty
Day: Tuesday
Book: Esther
Chapter: Nine
Memory Verse: Twenty-eight
Principle: It is important that we recite the history of God's blessings toward us because it builds faith and instills hope for generations to come.
Outline:

Verses 1-11 – On the day when the Jews were to be exterminated, the reverse occurred because they fought aggressively against their opponents.

Verses 12-17 – The king granted that they should have the following day as an additional opportunity to completely rid the country of their antagonists. The fact that they did not take the possessions of the people they destroyed proved that their motive was purely self-defense, not greed.

Verses 18-32 – An annual feast was established to commemorate the great deliverance that God gave them from their enemies.

Prayer Focus: Lord, help me never to forget all the blessings You pour into my life. Rather, may I always rejoice in reciting the testimonies of Your goodness to me. Amen.

Notes:

Spiritual Journal:

Week: Fifty
Day: Wednesday
Book: Esther
Chapter: Ten
Memory Verse: Three
Principle: God has a way of exalting those whose hearts are right before Him.
Outline:

> Verses 1-3 – Prosperity and blessing came upon the kingdom as Mordecai was elevated to a place of high authority.

Prayer Focus: Lord, may I always remember that promotion comes only from You. *Promotion cometh neither from the east, nor from the west, nor from the south. God is the judge: he puts down one, and sets up another.* (Psalm 75:6-7) Amen.

Notes:

Spiritual Journal:

Week: Fifty
Day: Thursday
Book: Ecclesiastes
Chapter: One
Memory Verse: One
Principle: Considering how insignificant one human's life, achievements, and knowledge are when compared to the vastness of the universe, it is impossible to find meaning in life without looking beyond the earthly realm.
Outline:
Verses 1-8 – Solomon considers the seemingly endless cycles of nature and wonders how any one human's life, no matter how much he accomplishes, can have any lasting importance. His conclusion is that life is vanity and insignificant.

Verses 9-11 – In the continuing saga of existence, it seems that no one life could possibly stand out as significantly unique; every cycle of life is just the same thing over again.

Verses 12-18 – In his quest for – and attainment of – great wisdom and knowledge, Solomon hoped to find a significant niche; however, he concluded that his mental achievements brought him only sorrow – not satisfaction.

Prayer Focus: Lord, help me to see life and living on a grand enough scale that I cannot be self-satisfied and self-centered in my existence. I don't ask to be frustrated with life; I simply ask to be healthily uncomfortable with myself. Amen.
Notes:

Spiritual Journal:

Week: Fifty
Day: Friday
Book: Ecclesiastes
Chapter: Two
Memory Verse: Twenty-four
Principle: In light of an existence that is marked with insignificance and frustration, it is only the graciousness of God's favor which gives essence to life.
Outline:
> Verses 1-11 – Solomon sought after pleasure, possessions, and prosperity in his quest for satisfaction and meaning in life; however, he found that all these things left him irreparably empty.
>
> Verses 12-16 – After pursuing wisdom and education, Solomon concluded that the brilliant are as easily forgotten after death as are the foolish and ignorant.
>
> Verses 17-23 – Solomon despaired over the hard work involved in amassing wealth, knowing that it must be left behind for another generation who might lose it all through foolishness or laziness.
>
> Verses 24-26 – He concluded that enjoying the blessing of God upon the simple things of life is the greatest significance in life and living.

Prayer Focus: Lord, help me to always recognize and appreciate Your hand upon my life and to acknowledge the meaning and significance You place upon my human existence. Amen.
Notes:

Spiritual Journal:

Week: Fifty-one
Day: Monday
Book: Ecclesiastes
Chapter: Three
Memory Verse: One
Principle: In God's over-all scheme, everything fits into its own time and place so that His ultimate purpose is fulfilled.
Outline:
Verses 1-8 – Everything – even seemingly contradictory things – all fit into God's master plan.

Verses 9-15 – God has placed an awareness of the eternal nature of things in the heart of man so that he is not satisfied with himself unless he is able to see his existence and his labors as part of God's extensive plan.

Verses 16-22 – Solomon recognized that our lives are all transitory, like the lives of the brute beasts; however, he also realized that man (unlike the animals) was subject to judgment for both his evil and his righteousness. Realizing this, he concluded that it is best for man to live his life so that he is happy and pleased with his own activities and accomplishments.

Prayer Focus: Lord, may I live each day with no personal regrets, knowing that I have lived each moment to the fullest of its potential and served You as completely as possible in all my actions. Amen.
Notes:

Spiritual Journal:

Week: Fifty-one
Day: Tuesday
Book: Ecclesiastes
Chapter: Four
Memory Verse: Nine
Principle: In all the futile relations based on oppression, envy, greed, and fleeting popularity, a true friend's support is vitally significant.
Outline:

> Verses 1-3 – When reviewing the seeming universality of oppression and abuse, Solomon concluded that those who are already dead and out from under this cruelty are better than those who are still enduring it; better yet, he concluded, are those who are never to be born to experience mortality.
>
> Verses 4-6 – Human desire for possessions and advancement is as empty as trying to catch hold of the wind.
>
> Verses 7-8 – Selfish efforts with no thought of sharing one's gain are fruitless.
>
> Verses 9-12 – Companionship yields immeasurable security and satisfaction.
>
> Verses 13-16 – Even in all the accolades of the rags-to-riches story, one's acclaim is only temporary and short-lived; in the end, it is also vanity.

Prayer Focus: Lord, may I have true friends and be a true friend to others. Amen.
Notes:

Spiritual Journal:

Week: Fifty-one

Day: Wednesday

Book: Ecclesiastes

Chapter: Five

Memory Verse: Ten

Principle: Satisfaction in life does not come from the things we own but from the fulfillment we accomplish in our obtaining them and our stewardship over them as well as in the relationship we have with the God who has allowed us to have those things.

Outline:

Verses 1-7 – There can be pitfalls in our attempts to find purpose and fulfillment in life even when we try to do so by following a spiritual approach. Making imprudent vows can bring us into religious bondage rather than godly liberty.

Verses 8-9 – Those who oppress their subjects are likely to be oppressed by those who have authority over them.

Verses 10-17 – Obtaining wealth is not fulfilling; riches bring with them parasites who prey upon those who hold the money. The truth is that just as we came into the world with an empty hand, so will we go out of this world.

Verses 18-19 – Fulfillment in life is to be able to earn one's own way and be content with what he has and to have activities that bring him inner satisfaction.

Prayer Focus: Lord, may I never lose focus upon the true goal in life – a heart that prospers more than a hand that grasps for possessions. Amen.

Notes:

Spiritual Journal:

Week: Fifty-one

Day: Thursday

Book: Ecclesiastes

Chapter: Six

Memory Verse: Eleven

Principle: In his pitiable state of not being able to find true fulfillment in life, the question arises, "What value is a man's life?"

Outline:

Verses 1-6 – Even though a man may achieve all the great goals in life – wealth, prestige, many children, long life – if he fails to find inner peace, his life is worth less than that of an aborted baby.

Verses 7-9 – Since all we work to accomplish simply feeds our outer man rather than nourishing our spiritual man, there is no significant difference between the man of standing and the social outcast.

Verses 10-12 – Solomon questions if there is anyone who can give meaning to man's existence.

Prayer Focus: Lord, I know that it is only through a vital relationship with You that my life will have any meaning. Help me never to lose perspective of that fact. Amen.

Notes:

Spiritual Journal:

Week: Fifty-one
Day: Friday
Book: Ecclesiastes
Chapter: Seven
Memory Verse: Twenty-nine
Principle: Man's vanity is not God's fault. He established a fulfilling plan for each man's life, but we have erred in following after our own schemes.
Outline:
> Verses 1-7 – Solomon expresses his despair in saying that he finds more satisfaction in mourning than in rejoicing and in being scolded than in laughter.
>
> Verses 8-10 – For Solomon, there was no such thing as the "good old days."
>
> Verses 11-14 – In all his questioning, Solomon repeatedly comes back to the conclusion that wisdom holds the key to finding meaning in life and that such wisdom must be grounded in an understanding of God and His ways.
>
> Verses 15-18 – Solomon suggests a life of moderation focused on the fear of the Lord which, he tells us in other contexts, is the beginning of wisdom.
>
> Verses 19-29 – In his quest for wisdom, Solomon found only one abiding truth: God has a plan for man to live a fulfilling and satisfying life, and it is only man's fault if he fails to find and experience it.

Prayer Focus: Lord, lead me into a healthy fear of the Lord, which will produce true wisdom in my life and lead me into a truly fulfilled and satisfied life. Amen.
Notes:

Spiritual Journal:

Week: Fifty-two

Day: Monday

Book: Ecclesiastes

Chapter: Eight

Memory Verse: Seventeen

Principle: God is infinite, and we will never be able to fully understand Him and explore the fathomless dimensions of His wisdom.

Outline:

> Verses 1-13 – Even the wise man with his wisdom and the king with his power do not know when death will come, nor do they have power over it. It is only those who fear the Lord who can have confidence in the face of death.

> Verses 14-17 – Perplexed by the inequities of life, Solomon turned to pleasure and the pursuit of wisdom in his vain quest for solace and answers.

Prayer Focus: Lord, help me to continue to be encouraged as I seek to know You and understand Your way. May I not be discouraged by the surface realities I encounter in the world around me. Amen.

Notes:

Spiritual Journal:

Week: Fifty-two
Day: Tuesday
Book: Ecclesiastes
Chapter: Nine
Memory Verse: Eighteen
Principle: Although the sinful fallen nature of our world often seems to overpower and negate the benefits of wisdom and righteousness, we must remember that the righteous and the wise, along with all their works, are in the hand of God. (Vs.1)
Outline:

Verses 1-2 – Solomon contemplated the inequity in a world where good things happen to bad people while bad things happen to good people.

Verses 3-6 – In a seeming reversal of an opinion expressed earlier, Solomon concludes that it is better to live than to die even if it is a life in a world of inequity and injustice.

Verses 7-10 – Solomon concluded that it is advisable to celebrate life even if we recognize that our days are full of vanity; there is no second chance after death comes.

Verses 11-18 – In our inequitable world, neither skill, strength, wisdom, nor understanding guarantee men success; rather, a universal evil seems to befall all men. One example that particularly impressed Solomon was the case of a wise man whose accomplishments were dismissed because of his poverty, leading Solomon to conclude that sin can overrule much good.

Prayer Focus: Lord, may I have the spiritual eyes to see beyond the injustices and inequities of my world and recognize that Your hand is upon me. Amen.
Notes:

Spiritual Journal:

Week: Fifty-two
Day: Wednesday
Book: Ecclesiastes
Chapter: Ten
Memory Verse: Two
Principle: The wise man with a spirit-controlled temperament keeps his emotions and imaginations in check; the foolish man is unable to control the reins of his soul.
Outline:

Verses 1-2 – Even a little foolishness can undo a wise man's reputation.

Verses 3-4 – A foolish man deserves no respect.

Verses 5-7 – When he observed inferiors ruling over their superiors, Solomon recognized it as added proof that the world is full of inequities.

Verses 8-10 – The fact that so many people's livelihoods are the cause of their disablements or deaths again reinforces his conclusion concerning the injustices of life.

Verses 11-15 – A foolish man's words are as dangerous as a venomous serpent's bite.

Verses 16-17 – Selfish leaders curse a country, but wise leaders bless it.

Verses 18-19 – There must be caution given to understand the difference between enjoying life and taking life so easily that we allow our resources to deteriorate.

Verse 20 – There is no such thing as a secret.

Prayer Focus: Lord, may I experience spiritual control over my mind that will yield life and peace.(Romans 8:6) Amen.

Week: Fifty-two
Day: Thursday
Book: Ecclesiastes
Chapter: Eleven
Memory Verse: Five
Principle: Faith is following the words of God even though we do not logically understand all His ways.
Outline:

Verses 1-6 – Realizing that we cannot understand all the depths of God's ways, we must live by faith, abiding by all the principles we know – whether we fully understand them or not. We must be assured that that we will be rewarded even though we do not know exactly how, when, or where.

Verses 7-8 – Although Solomon concludes that the days which come in our old age are vanity and the days of our youth are also vanity, he admonishes us to rejoice in both our youth and old age. With the faith of God in our lives, we can be optimistic in a pessimistic world.

Prayer Focus: Lord, may it be my testimony that I have lived by faith, not by sight. Amen.
Notes:

Spiritual Journal:

Week: Fifty-two
Day: Friday
Book: Ecclesiastes
Chapter: Twelve
Memory Verse: Thirteen
Principle: The total purpose of man – beyond amassing wealth, constructing great civic
projects, indulging in pleasures, attaining wisdom and knowledge – is simply to
keep the commandments of God.
Outline:
Verses 1-7 – Solomon admonished his readers to begin their pursuit of God early
in life, not to wait until their lives were spent and their bodies feeble.
Verses 8-12 – Although he still affirmed that life is emptiness and vanity,
Solomon purposed to bring rhyme and reason to it through his wise
teachings. The summation of his intellectual quest was that one could
weary himself through the study of even the most enlightened books and
that there was only one simple injunction which concluded the matter.
Verses 13-14 – If a man respects and obeys God, God will eventually balance out
every inequity in his life.
Prayer Focus: Lord, no matter how cloudy the skies may get and how foggy my path may
be, may I never lose my direction in life. May I never lose sight of Your hand at
work in my situation. Amen.
Notes:

Spiritual Journal:

Teach All Nations Mission

Teach All Nations Mission (TAN) is a global evangelical educational ministry birthed from the teaching ministries of Delron and Peggy Shirley. The name for Teach All Nations Mission was chosen to carefully indicate the exact heart of the Shirleys' mission. TAN's commitment is to establish a solid biblical foundation in national pastors and leaders so they can help enrich their own people. This vision is being accomplished by holding national leadership conferences and publishing and distributing Christian teaching materials in English and their local languages.

Someone accurately observed concerning the revival that is occurring in many parts of our world today that it is a mile wide but only an inch deep – the result of energetic evangelism by both missionaries and local Christians. Sadly, there is a marked shortage of teachers who are taking the next step in fulfilling our Lord's directive to teach them how to observe all that He has commanded. Therefore, Teach All Nations Mission has literally taken the words of Christ from Matthew 28:19, "Teach all nations," as its motto and mission statement.

TAN's commitment is to deepen that revival by training the pastors and leaders who then go back and strengthen their congregations. TAN pays for the travel and lodging of handpicked leaders because Delron and Peggy want to invest into their lives but know that these third-world saints could never afford to come at their own expense. TAN always provides the meals for all the guests during these conferences. The ministry also furnishes solid Christian literature in their local language or in English for those who understand the language.

Delron and Peggy realize that the challenge is much bigger than what they can accomplish in person; therefore, they have determined to expand the scope of their vision. One area of expansion includes a scholarship fund that will allow selected individuals to obtain a formal education in solid Christian colleges and Bible schools or through correspondence courses. The ministry has also assisted in building a Christian school in Zimbabwe and a Bible college in Nepal. Additionally, Teach All Nations assists the pastors and leaders they work with in times of need such as the tsunami in Sri Lanka, the earthquake in Nepal, and hurricanes in Belize and in the Turks and Caicos Islands. More recently, the ministry supported suffering Christians in twelve different nations who lost their source of income during the shutdowns during the COVID-19 pandemic.

Your gifts to and prayers for Teach All Nations will help the Shirleys continue their outreach to Christian leadership around the world.

Teach All Nations Mission
3210 Cathedral Spires
Colorado Springs, CO 80904
719-685-9999
www.teachallnationsmission.com
teachallnations@msn.com

Books by Delron & Peggy Shirley

Bingo, a Fresh Look at Grace
Christmas Thoughts
Cornerstones of Faith
Daily Bible Study Series (Five-Volume Set)
Daily Ditties from Delron's Desk
(Eight Volumes Available)
Doctor Livingstone, I Presume
Don't Leave Home Without It
Finally, My Brethren
Getting More UMPH out of Your Bible
Going Deeper in Jesus
The Great Commission – Doable
The IN Factors
In This Sign Conquer
Interface
Israel, Key to Human Destiny
The Last Enemy
Lessons Along the Way
Lessons from the Life of David
Living for the End Times
Maturing into the Full Stature of Jesus Christ
Maximum Impact
No Longer Bound
The Non-Conformer's Trilogy
Of Kings and Prophets
Passion for the Harvest
People Who Make A Difference
Positioned for Blessing and Power
Problem People of the Bible
Seeds and Harvest
The Seventh Man at the Well
So Send I You
So, You Wanna be a Preacher
Thirty-, Sixty-, One-Hundred-Fold
Tread Marks
Turning the World Upside Down and Back Again
Verse for the Day (Four Volumes Available)
Women for the Harvest
You'll be Darned to Heck
if You Don't Believe in Gosh
You Can Be Healed
Your Home Can Survive in the 21st Century
Your Part in the Grand Scheme of Things

Available at:
teachallnationsmission.com